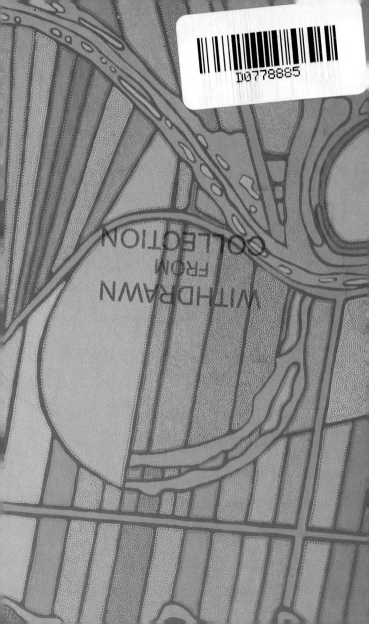

TOWARDS
—a Prairie—
ATONEMENT

TREVOR HERRIOT
Afterword by Norman Fleury

Printed and bound in Canada at Friesens.

COVER AND TEXT DESIGN: Duncan Campbell, University of Regina Press
COPY EDITOR: Dallas Harrison   PROOFREADER: Kristine Douaud
COVER AND INTERIOR ILLUSTRATIONS AND MAP: Trevor Herriot
ENDSHEETS: *Red River 1870s (beaded map)*, by David Garneau.
Acrylic on canvas, 122 × 153cm., 2006, collection of
the University of Saskatchewan.

Library and Archives Canada Cataloguing in Publication

Herriot, Trevor, author
Towards a prairie atonement / Trevor Herriot ; afterword by Norman Fleury.

(Regina collection)
Includes bibliographical references.
Issued also in electronic format.
ISBN 978-0-88977-454-4 (hardback).—ISBN 978-0-88977-455-1 (pdf).—
ISBN 978-0-88977-456-8 (html)

1. Métis—Manitoba—Ste. Madeleine—History. 2. Métis—Land tenure—
Manitoba—Ste. Madeleine—History. 3. Grassland ecology—Manitoba—
Ste. Madeleine. 4. Ste. Madeleine (Man.)—Ethnic relations—History.
5. Ste. Madeleine (Man.)—History. I. Title. II. Series: Regina collection

E99.M47H47 2016   971.27'400497   C2016-905703-8   C2016-905704-6

University of Regina Press
Saskatchewan, Canada, S4S 0A2
TEL: (306) 585-4758 FAX: (306) 585-4699
WEB: www.uofrpress.ca

10 9 8 7 6 5 4 3 2

We acknowledge the support of the Canada Council for the Arts for our publishing program.
We acknowledge the financial support of the Government of Canada. / Nous reconnaissons
l'appui financier du gouvernement du Canada. This publication was made possible through
Creative Saskatchewan's Creative Industries Production Grant Program.

*To those who take up
the work of reconciliation*

CONTENTS

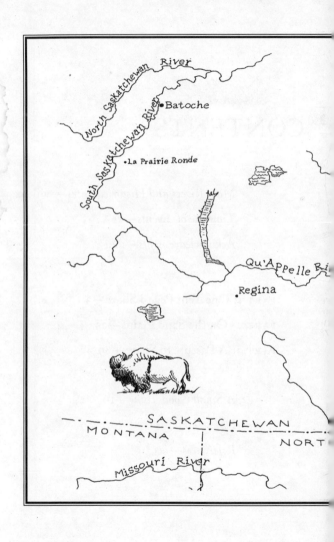

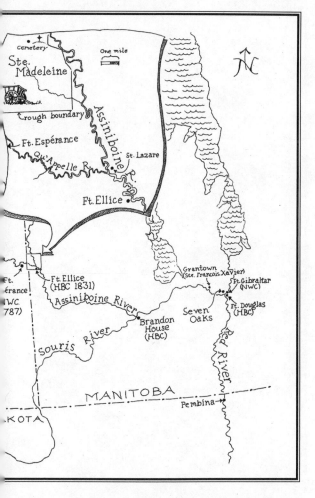

RIVERS AND HISTORICAL SITES IN

Towards a Prairie Atonement

TIMELINE *of* EVENTS

1600s–1700s: The fur trade brings thousands of European men to the Canadian northwest. French and Scottish traders begin to intermarry with Cree, Saulteaux, and Assiniboine women. The Métis of the Canadian plains trace their kinship from these origins.

1670: The English Crown grants the Hudson's Bay Company a charter over Rupert's Land—all lands draining into Hudson Bay.

1787: The North West Company opens Fort Espérance in the Qu'Appelle Valley just upstream of the confluence with the Assiniboine River.

1804: The trade war between the North West Company and Hudson's Bay Company begins.

1812: The Selkirk Colony is established at the Forks of the Red and Assiniboine rivers—the first non-Indigenous settlement on what was to become the Canadian plains.

1814: The Pemmican Proclamation is issued by Miles Macdonell, Governor of Assiniboia, at the bidding of Lord Selkirk and the Hudson's Bay Company, placing Métis independence and rights in jeopardy.

FALL OF 1815: Governor Semple arrives at the Selkirk Colony.

MAY 8, 1816: Cuthbert Grant leads a group of Métis men east to accompany a shipment of pemmican past the Selkirk Colony to North West Company men waiting for supplies at Lake Winnipeg. The Métis flag is flown for the first time.

JUNE 19, 1816: Grant's brigade is confronted by Semple and Selkirk settlers at Seven Oaks. The skirmish ends with twenty-two men dead.

JANUARY 10, 1817: Miles Macdonell retakes Fort Douglas (at present-day Winnipeg) for the Hudson's Bay Company.

1821: The North West Company and Hudson's Bay Company merge.

1820–60s: Métis buffalo hunting expeditions depart from the Red River.

1839: George Simpson is appointed governor of Rupert's Land and the Hudson's Bay Company.

1869: The government of Canada, the government of Great Britain, and the Hudson's Bay Company sign an agreement selling Rupert's Land to the Dominion of Canada. No one consults the thousands of Métis, First Nations, and settler people living in the region.

1869–70: At the Red River, Louis Riel and his followers seize Fort Garry and establish a provisional government, asserting the Métis claim on the newly established District of Assiniboia—in what comes to be called the first Riel Resistance.

1880s: The last wild buffalo are hunted down to a small remnant.

1885: Louis Riel is elected president of the North-West Territories provisional government; after the Battle of Batoche, he is taken prisoner, tried, and executed on November 16 at Regina.

1900–02: Métis families begin settling around a new Ste. Madeleine mission established north of Fort Ellice by Oblate Father DeCorby.

1935: The Canadian government responds to the dust bowl of the Dirty Thirties by passing the Prairie Farm Rehabilitation Act, thereby establishing a community pasture system across Manitoba and Saskatchewan.

1937-1938: The 250 Métis people living at Ste. Madeleine are told they will have to leave and resettle elsewhere because the land will be used for a new community pasture.

MARCH 2012: Stephen Harper's Conservative government ends the community pasture program, removing federal protection and programming for vulnerable grassland ecosystems.

ACKNOWLEDGEMENTS

One of the delights of reading a book is its physical presence in the hand—its size and heft, the tooth and shade of the paper stock, the way the inked words and images cast their shadows and set the negative space to vibrating. The small book has its own genius for concentrating the effect of each decision made by the editor and designer. Those decisions, when handled by staff at a small press, can sometimes produce a small book that binds its feel and appearance gracefully to the writer's text.

That was our shared hope when I began working with the University of Regina Press on this book: to create something that, while small compared with the magnitude of its themes, is crafted to be congruent with the voices it bears. We wanted to give readers a story of loss that is the right size to hold and ponder—but, more important, the right size to reconcile.

If it works and we manage to achieve some of that coherence between form and content, then the credit goes entirely to my editor Karen Clark, publisher and irrepressible force of nature Bruce Walsh, designer Duncan Campbell, managing editor Donna Grant, copy editor Dallas Harrison, and the rest of the team at the University of Regina Press. They have all been enthusiastic, professional, and inspired from first to last, but it was Karen's skills, sensitivity, and unflagging dedication to the project that brought it into the light of day. I owe her every gratitude for the extra effort and hours she took on.

If this narrative—bound to a particular piece of prairie but interleaved with the larger matter of how we suppressed an emergent communal land tenure system on the northern Great Plains—reads only as a lament, then I have failed. I will take the blame for that and any other shortcomings and missteps herein, but I have set my heart on telling a story that will inspire people to take a second look at what we all lost, and could yet restore, in our regard for more sophisticated and nuanced forms of land governance.

I am indebted to many people who have helped me to learn, think through, and articulate the subtleties that confound our comprehension of what has formed and what might reform our ways of owning and sharing land on the prairie. I want to especially acknowledge the tireless efforts and inspired leadership of North America's grassland conservationists, including my fellow travellers at Public Pastures–Public Interest.

Finally, and most emphatically, I offer my deep gratitude to Michif Elder, historian, and linguist Norman Fleury. His passion for his Michif language and people and confidence in their survival is in itself a testimony to the life that will endure and renew itself if we will but grant it room to flourish on these plains.

Whether we are indigenous or newcomer, today our tipis are held down by the same peg. Neither is going anywhere. The knowledge and the will needed to protect and save these places no longer belongs to one people or one tradition.

—*Cynthia Chambers and Narcisse Blood,*
"Love Thy Neighbour: Repatriating
Precarious Blackfoot Sites"

— PART I —

ONE TENT PEG TO SHARE

Well, make sure you don't take it all.

—Qu'Appelle Valley farmer to people
from Pasqua First Nation gathering
blackroot (echinacea) on his land

The longspur, white tail feathers flashing, exploded into flight at our feet and then settled a short distance away. We stooped to look briefly at the swirl of green shade hiding her four speckled eggs, warm and holy. The wind all around us was strung with the bells of chestnut-collared longspur song, but this was the first nest we came upon.

If there is a world more complete and vulnerable than the nest of a small bird tucked into grass, I have not seen it. Walking the edge of a treeless plain a thousand acres across, I had to remind myself that there was a forest a few paces away. Like the longspur nest, it was concealed, recessed into the prairie in a great wooded trench, half a mile wide and three hundred feet deep. Yesterday, a biologist told me a story about a bow hunter who just last year mounted a tree stand in this valley above some bait he put out to attract bears. The first morning he climbed up into the stand, the bears started to come at daylight, and before he could make a move he was surrounded by forty-three of them. He was treed for much of the day waiting for the last ones to leave.

Down in the wooded bottomlands, the large mammals are faring well, but up here on this sandy plain the smaller creatures that depend on grass are rapidly thinning out. It is thus all the way from the Red River in Winnipeg to the foothills of the Rocky Mountains. Most of the remaining longspurs and other endangered grassland species are farther to the southwest where the Milk and Frenchman rivers drain the largest stretches of native grass on the northern Great Plains. This outlier of prairie, containing two publicly owned community pastures of native grass and oak/poplar savannah, is a remote daughter cut off from her mother by hundreds of miles of cultivation.

For twenty years I have been making trips like this one, out onto the scattered archipelago of native prairie islands surrounded by a sea of cash crops, sometimes escaping from and sometimes searching for the hubris in our regard for the land, the arrogance that puts it to the plow and drives the birds away.

The pasture with the longspur nest is right on the Saskatchewan-Manitoba border and a few miles north of the Trans-Canada Highway, three hours east of my home in Regina. I caught a ride with Branimir Gjetvaj, a grassland naturalist and photographer working on a photography book that will feature the endangered grasslands of Canada's community pastures. As rare and ecologically important as coastal rainforest, and hosting thirty-one species at risk, they are officially listed by the World Commission on Protected Areas under the International Union for Conservation of Nature (IUCN) as lands that Canada has made a commitment to protect. In the spring of 2012, however, the Stephen Harper government abandoned that commitment on behalf of all Canadians by ending the program and removing federal protection from these vulnerable landscapes.

That single legislative decision, destroying a grazing commons that was a model of conservation and sustainability, has set grassland conservationists and ranchers scrambling to find a way to prevent the privatization of more than eighty large grassland remnants in Saskatchewan and Manitoba that make up a land base of 9,300 square kilometres—nearly twice the size of Prince Edward Island.

I was recruited into the fray by a brown envelope that arrived in my mailbox shortly after the announcement. It was a package of information on the conservation programming of the pastures, with an anonymous note from a federal employee, asking me to help defend the birds and other creatures being placed at risk. I began talking to conservationists, and within a month we had formed a new advocacy group we called Public Pastures–Public Interest. The neo-liberal version of Canada created by the Harper Conservatives—a dark tunnel in which privileged white people slashed social services and environmental regulations and privatized the public good to cut taxes for elites and corporations—had always seemed just off stage, but now I was walking into it in the company of a couple of friends and some people I barely knew.

Four years into that tunnel, we believe we are seeing some light ahead. We have nearly fifty organizations and hundreds of supporters on our side, and we are meeting regularly with ranchers, environmental groups, First Nations organizations, and MPs to discuss ways to keep the pastures public lands managed for a mix of conservation and livestock grazing. Not long ago, during a week in which we lost a couple of key board members, including a close friend and a young First Nations man who hunts on the pastures, I was skimming through a chapter near the end of Thomas Berry's *Dream of the Earth*—an old book I often thumb through when I am trying to find my way in the dark.[1] At the bottom of a page discussing the need for Indigenous and non-Indigenous communities to connect by fostering the cultural traditions of First Peoples, I had many years ago scribbled something in the margin: "'The Blackfoot and the white people here now share one tent peg.' From Narcisse Blood, as told to me by Cynthia Chambers."

Cynthia, a writer friend and university professor from Lethbridge, wanted to introduce Narcisse and me. I knew him by reputation as a Blackfoot Elder from the Blood Reserve and a filmmaker who had much to say about the role of culture and spirituality in honouring the grassland world that had fed his people for uncounted generations. Over the years Narcisse and I had connected once or twice on email, but the timing had never worked out for a meeting. Then, in February 2015, it seemed as though we would finally get together. A phone message came early in the day from a friend, Michele Sereda: "Hi, Trevor. Sorry for the short notice, but I am working with Narcisse Blood and some others on a project. He reads your work and would like to meet you to talk about grassland. We are just heading out to Piapot for the day but could meet you at the Hotel Sask lounge at seven. Text or call me back."

I tried calling Michele right away and didn't get an answer so sent her a text message saying I would love to talk to Narcisse about grassland. That night I went to the lounge of the hotel and waited. An hour passed by. I called Michele again but got no answer. When I got home, the phone rang. It was my eldest daughter, Kate, who often worked with Michele in theatre. She was crying, barely able to speak: "Dad, Michele Sereda died in a car accident today."

Narcisse, Michele, Michael Green (co-founder of Calgary's One Yellow Rabbit theatre), and dancer Lacy Morin-Desjarlais had all been killed that morning, as well as the driver of the truck they collided with on the icy highway to Piapot First Nation north of Regina.

In the days to come, I tried to learn more about the project the four artists had been working on. I knew Michele and her fearless commitment to collaborative processes and cross-cultural expressions from working with her on a play ten years earlier. Since then she had become a fixture in Indigenous theatre, inspiring young people to use the stage to bring their world to life in voice, movement, and story. As the weeks passed by, all I could find out was that she had brought the group together to create a performance piece aimed at uniting Indigenous and non-Indigenous people under treaty and with shared responsibilities to the land and one another.

At the memorial for Michele, several hundred people filling three galleries of the T. C. Douglas building's atrium, we wept together for the loss of her vibrancy, her unbounded enthusiasm, and her good heart. During the reception afterward, we filed by a screen showing film clips of Michele and then past tables with memorabilia, including her bulletin board, taken as it was, from her house. I glanced at it, smiling at the array of notes and reminders from a life filled with creativity and passion, and my eyes fell on a yellow sticky note. It was my phone number and a reminder to call.

Throughout that late winter and spring, Canadians would hear again and again about the need for decolonization and reconciliation between Indigenous and non-Indigenous people as the Truth and Reconciliation Commission moved towards its conclusion. An artist-activist who had moved freely in both communities, Michele had been doing the work of reconciliation for years. To those of us who admired her courage and believed in what she was doing, that work suddenly seemed much more difficult but also much more urgent.

More than reconciliation, in someone like Michele there is a longing to come together, not to merge but to meet one another on level ground, distinct and equal, and to sing and dance together, sharing without taking. There is an English verb for this coming together when one side has more to give up and let go of—to *atone*. The power of *at-one-ment* has been covered up by the ashes of propitiatory fires from old religious narratives about an angry God demanding sacrifice for sin. Yet it is true: "sin" or estrangement is part of being human, and there is sacrifice in the work that brings us nearer to the place where we can be at one with the land and with one another across, but with deep respect for, all creaturely, cultural, and racial distinctions.

The first thing to sacrifice in coming together is our own agendas and designs, our knowing just what the world needs. I almost always stumble over my own purposes and preconceptions when I work with Indigenous people on a project. No matter how hard I try not to trip, I often do, and I look back later at the work and realize I might have committed that "greatest treason—to do the right deed for the wrong reason." For a time I lose my courage. Afraid of being clumsy, of being someone who takes and uses without proper respect and with too much desire in my heart, I swear off all attempts.

At the memorial someone said that Michele was never afraid of failing, and sometimes she did it spectacularly. We all laughed and knew it was true, part of what made her so easy to love. Returning home from the service, I knew it was fear of failure that had kept me from pursuing the friendship with Narcisse—fear of my own motives spoiling the effort.

I decided I would try again. I would make mistakes—my desire to save native grassland and its creatures would get in the way and make it hard to listen—but I would try anyway, and in the trying maybe some small good thing would happen.

God knows, the prairie world beyond the green shade of the longspur nest is waiting for atonement of one kind or another. The choices we make as the upright primates who put the "anthro" in the Anthropocene will determine whether we are here to be part of that coming together, but it will happen with or without us. Such thoughts are born of sitting in rooms. Out on the Sand Plains, with a nest to crouch beside, all theories and apprehensions fade as the genius of the place conjures up memories of being at home in the world. It happens whenever I come to this part of the prairie where the back and forth between upland and bottomland spreads fingers of grassland around bowls of forest—aspen bluff and speargrass above, sweeping coulees of bur oak and bluestem below—all of it woven together in contrapuntal melodies that carry notes from the continent's boreal crown to the grassland at its heart.

The angle of light and the signature of landform in a place may stir our deepest dreams of home, but for the descendants of settlers notions of belonging are tangled with family claims to the prairie. In the 1880s, letters describing the Qu'Appelle River country went east and drew my Scottish ancestors to homestead north of the valley. My mother, eighty-nine and the last surviving member of her generation, can't recall what she had for lunch or who visited her yesterday, but she remembers the Métis families stopping to camp beneath the maples next to their yard where the Kaposvar Creek empties into the Qu'Appelle.

At this latitude, changes in the weather generally come from the west, but changes caused by people have tended to come from the east. The marks of all that has transformed the prairie in the past two centuries are oldest here on the eastern rim, where grass and forest interdigitate. Ghosts of abandoned frontiers, they surround this island of grass with the scars of extraction, transportation, and displacement: the remains of a pemmican depot from the 1780s, a Hudson's Bay Company fort that closed a century later, a Red River cart trail heading northwest, a First Nations reserve, an abandoned rail line, a potash mine, a Métis settlement, and farmyards displaying old plowshares and the names of early homesteaders.

Beneath each of those wounds is a midden of stories bearing layers of loss and suffering that settlers too quickly lacquered over with tales of butter down the well and hogs in the horseradish. Colonialism, we have learned too late, is an utterly unreliable narrator.

The work of decolonizing, of atonement, begins with the act of recognizing and honouring what was and is native but has been evicted from the land—native plants and animals but the original peoples, cultures, and languages too.

In Kluane National Park or the Great Bear Rainforest, this kind of loss is harder to see. Degradation and suffering are there too, but the traces are disguised beneath the magnitude of nature and the fantasy of "the pristine." We all need to protect and experience our remaining wild lands, today more than ever, but parks and reserves represent a small portion of our planet. Most of us live in landscapes that have been greatly altered by human agency—agricultural, industrial, or urban. Nature struggles to survive at the edges of a corn field or in a creek running through the city, but it is still there and just as worthy of our attention and defence.

Good things happen when we go to such places. It is not hard to find a piece of land degraded but not yet annihilated by human activity. Walk through a place isolated or damaged by the extractive impulses of our species, and, if you are quiet enough, attentive enough, you will be able to read its narrative of loss. The gift of any place, in soil and leaf and limb, remains remote until you expose your soft human belly to its brokenness. You may worry that, if you let down your guard and acknowledge what is missing, the sadness will overtake you. And it may for a spell, but if you stay your thoughts will soon enough turn to the survivors. A kind of intimacy settles in, dissolving the sorrow in gratitude for what remains and hope for what could yet be restored, reconciled. Canada's prairie landscapes— still rowdy with the old life, still sanctuaries of wildness, but clearly in decline and need of more compassion and attention—give themselves readily to such a practice.

Pieces of grassland cut off from the main are suffering all over this continent, and there are people letting these places move them. Some live and work there in a tradition of stewardship that runs back to their great-grandparents; others come from away, take the risk of getting to know an ecology in crisis, and then see what can be done to help. If they get cranky when reflecting on what has happened in the passing of two centuries here, it is partly because they know that, like most who live on the prairie, they owe at least some of their privilege and comfort to sodbusting settlers and the agricultural economy they founded on stolen land.

The triumph of Canada's rapid settlement of the plains was that it created tens of thousands of freehold farmers by taking a million and a half square miles of land chartered to a corporate monopoly, the Hudson's

Bay Company (HBC), and then distributing it to grateful, hard-working peasants in 160-acre parcels. It was a bold experiment in democratizing land ownership, an important egalitarian departure from the decaying feudal systems of the Old World, and it brought prosperity to the mosaic of displaced Europeans who largely formed prairie settler culture.

The tragedy of that undertaking was in not respecting and including the Indigenous people and their legitimate and wise ways of sharing the prairie. That foundational exclusion hurt all of us, not only First Nations and Métis people, because it decoupled land-use decisions from established and emergent forms of land tenure that would have enabled us to get beyond the usual binary between private and public ownership. A third way, found in Indigenous perspectives on land and refined in Métis concepts of land governance, offered—and could still offer—the basis of a more sophisticated regulatory model that would respect and conserve long-term community interest in the well-being of the land.

Private land ownership on the Great Plains applied technology to spawn miracles of agricultural production and private wealth since settlement, but the exertions of public interest in the land, as represented in government policy and Crown land regulation, have failed to protect the common wealth and health that we share in nature, with its abundance of clean air, water, and fertile soil. Both sides, private and public interest, are too vulnerable to the economics of endless growth and the demands of distant markets for cheap fuel and food. When the commonwealth is bartered away to drive up GDP in a nation where almost everyone—"rural" people included—is now living a de facto urban existence, the public interest represented in government is powerless to defend the community. Having assented to the article of faith that we must feed growing populations with fewer farmers producing higher yields, traditional politics has no answer to the question of how we produce food without ruining our land and water. All ideologies founder at the farm gate, and sooner or later the private interest in land becomes concentrated again in the corporation.

We live in an era when the prairie is veering back into corporate hands. Oil, gas, and potash corporations are setting the agenda for provincial land-use policy. Investment companies, pension plans, and large farmer-investor hybrids are rushing to purchase what is becoming one of the scarcest commodities on the planet—arable land. Governments are selling Crown land, farmers wanting to retire are cashing out, and financial advisers are telling their clients that prairie farmland is an "inflation-protected asset that produces income." Even what we call the "family farm" now often involves a million-dollar corporation that seeds and harvests tens of thousands of acres.

Meanwhile, too many prairie people, Indigenous and non-Indigenous, are living with industrialized, degraded landscapes and undrinkable water. Surprisingly, many farm people don't see it that way. Not long ago I had a phone call from a farmer who raises cattle and crops in the transitional zone between Aspen Parkland and Boreal Forest. We agreed that city people and our governments do almost nothing to compensate or encourage farmers or ranchers who conserve habitat on their land. Well-spoken and philosophical, he said that our industrialized agricultural practices are not sustainable and that many species are being hurt. He worries about the bees, both tame and wild, suffering from the neo-nicotinoid seed coating on the GMO canola that he plants. He spoke at some length about how commodity agriculture drives farmers to bulldoze and plow up habitat, yet before he was finished he told me he believed that on balance we have done a fair job of keeping natural landscapes on the prairie during the past century.

Though I have heard this seesaw of logic many times before, it caught me off guard. A man of good heart, who lives on the land and cares for it while he grows food for the rest of us, chooses to celebrate the half-full part of a glass that in fact is less than one-fifth full. Is it that we can't take a lot of reality? Or is it some pathology in our collective regard for history and civilization—the same one that has historians declaring that ancient Britain's greatest achievement was clearing the wildwood to make room for the social advances that come with the raising of sheep and the growing of cereal crops?

I paused and then muttered a half-hearted response, not wanting to be disagreeable at the end of a pleasant conversation. Here is what I didn't say.

If the glass were merely half empty, I would be happy to raise it in a toast, but you and I share a province where 80 per cent of the natural cover on the prairie has been scraped away and more of it is disappearing every year down the throat of a beast whose appetite cannot be satisfied. Only 3.5 per cent of the native grassland in Canada's Prairie Ecozone has any form of protection.[2] Some endangered species are now at less than 10 per cent of their populations forty years ago. The little that remains, our fragments of old-growth prairie, are every bit as diverse and irreplaceable as Canada's last refuges of old-growth forest, but they are under siege from forces ranging from privatization and cultivation to resource extraction and ranchette development. And the worst of it is that damned few people seem to notice.

We might be able to hide the truth from ourselves, but the animals know. These days cities on the Great Plains attract more birds, jackrabbits, and ground squirrels than the surrounding farmland. Poor as it is, the urban habitat is better. But it is not only wild creatures we are missing.

The private interest that founded prairie settler life has been shanghaied and thrown aboard the train of corporatized and denatured agriculture. If the public interest constituted in our governments is powerless to stop it, then what will?

There *is* that third kind of interest—the community—that for thousands of years helped to balance the well-being of the individual and the well-being of the land. Eventually, it evolved into the sharing of grass, what the Red River Métis called *le privilège de couper le foin*—literally "the right to cut the hay" or "the hay privilege." The Métis, I believe, were helping to bring a balance to land-use practices, but their experiment was cut down before it had a chance to mature further and inform western Canada's agricultural economy.

From the outset of the fur trade in the seventeenth century, the long-term interests of local communities all over the northern plains have been sold down the river to industries serving distant markets. That barter has done great damage to entire nations of people, and the same disregard for land and community continues today to send our young men and women into industries that have found new ways to mine the prairie and destroy our human connections to each other and the land. True community governance has been missing or severely weakened for some time now, though remnants of it did thrive among settlers too for a generation or so after treaties, residential schools, and homesteading forced the Indigenous versions underground.

In hardship and calamity, a sense of the commonwealth of the community has revived for a spell in prairie places, only to recede when the promise of individual prosperity overwhelmed the pragmatism of shared interest. Although much diminished, that third element—moderating private interest out of concern for the long-term well-being of the land and human communities—can be a strong conserving influence because it is necessarily local and tied up with local values and economies. It arose when farmers first formed dairy and grain cooperatives to get fair prices for their produce, when they established their own telephone companies connecting farmstead to farmstead with copper wire along fencelines, and when the dust bowl of the 1930s stopped every farmer in his field with a reminder that nature is in charge.

In the first drought cycle after a couple of decades of settlement and tillage, the prairie soil was travelling on the wind in dark blizzards, sandblasting settler shacks, and piling in drifts along fencelines clotted with tumbleweeds. By 1937, the federal government decided to intervene with some soil and water conservation measures under a new government agency called the Prairie Farm Rehabilitation Administration (PFRA). It would work with local communities and the prairie provinces to preserve grasslands, return cropped land to grass cover, conserve surface water and soil, and provide irrigation systems. And it would establish community pastures run by the federal Ministry of Agriculture for decades to come, providing local farm families with affordable grazing and prairie wildlife with a network of refuges where they would survive into the twenty-first century. In this way, the Canadian government unwittingly restored a faint shadow of the grassland dispensation that had existed since the retreat of the glaciers and that colonization had rapidly erased.

The closer you look at the islands of native grassland ecology that community pastures protect, the more you will find human stories that have the power to renew our relationships to the prairie and help us come to understand community interest. Like the nest of a small bird tucked into a circle of grass, one of those stories is hidden away in a sunlit sandy plain seven thousand years old and enclosed by the Spy Hill–Ellice community pasture straddling the Saskatchewan-Manitoba border. With the guidance of an Elder who has not only the knowledge and right to share the story but also the borne-in-the-blood connection that will not let us close our ears, the pages that follow take another look at the forces that squandered the gifts of the prairie. Along the way, the narrative re-examines Métis history and land tenure through the lens of the Red River people who retreated to this grassland remnant long before it became a community pasture.

No story can match a walk beneath skies ringing with longspur and pipit song, but the right story might remind us why such things still matter today and how protecting them can bring prairie people and all Canadians one step closer to atonement, one step closer to a restored covenant with the land and the peoples who have known it well and long.

— PART 2 —

ON THE SAND PLAINS

"How do you talk about loss? There is pain in the story, so for a long time people didn't talk about it. But now we do."

As his truck rumbles south on a gravel road, Norman Fleury gestures with a hand above the steering wheel. An open palm tilts towards miles of prairie, holding all that is in his mind: stories his grandmother told him, the language of his birth, and a desire to be fair and honest in explaining what happened on the plot of land just ahead of us.

The Spy Hill–Ellice community pasture is approximately 160 square kilometres of Aspen Parkland prairie straddling the Manitoba-Saskatchewan border, near the town of St. Lazare and the juncture of the Qu'Appelle and Assiniboine rivers. The road we are on runs parallel to the border a kilometre inside Manitoba. This tract of publicly managed grassland, along with its sister the Ellice–Archie pasture (150 square kilometres) a short distance to the south, represents the last large expanse of upland native prairie in this corner of the northern Great Plains. There are rare birds here whose breeding population is so isolated their nearest counterparts are 200 kilometres or more south and west.

Norman agreed to take me to the pasture on this morning in late May 2015. Branimir follows in his Subaru, likely still grumbling about the light or my peanut butter sandwich smelling up the cab. Hating peanut butter is a mild handicap for an outdoor photographer, but midday light is a deal breaker. We will have to see what the evening brings, he tells me, or camp overnight to shoot at dawn.

The pasture is the core of what local farmers still call the Sand Plains—leftover land whose poor soil attracted few, if any, white homesteaders. Sand Plains history is a narrative of men and women as hardy as poplar trees, surviving, even thriving, on a prairie that agronomists dismiss as unproductive. A century and a half before the Canadian government drew lines around the Spy Hill–Ellice community pasture, before the four strands of federal barbed wire enclosed it, a new and resilient prairie people were living here and at places like it throughout the watersheds of the lower Qu'Appelle and Assiniboine rivers. Neither the original race nor the colonizers, yet bearing some of each in their flesh and customs, these early modern dwellers on the plains, refugees displaced from Batoche, the Red River, and elsewhere, spoke the language, sang the songs, and told the stories that their fur-trading ancestors first voiced in the prairie world.

This morning, when we met for a late breakfast at a restaurant in the town of Binscarth, Norman introduced us to an old friend, a Mr. Genaille, who works as a grain buyer these days. His father was a great speaker of Michif, the Métis language rooted in a mix of Cree and French, still spoken in pockets of Manitoba, Saskatchewan, and North Dakota. As they visited and laughed at memories, bits of Michif spilling into their English, Norman began to talk about the origins of the language. His explanation, one he learned from his grandmother as a child, would fit well in one of the books he has written in Michif or in the undergrad language classes he teaches at the University of Saskatchewan.

"I asked my *koohkoom*, I said, 'Where did the language come from?' And she said, 'Why are you asking me that?'

"Nobody asks where their language comes from because you are born with the language. But she said, 'You come tomorrow morning, and I will tell you.' I used to go there every morning for breakfast—we shared the same little farm. 'You come and eat tomorrow morning. I will think about it.' She didn't want to just give me any old answer—it had to be the right one.

"The next day she said, 'You know, grandson, when God created the world'—you see the old people always gave everything that spiritual context—'overseas there are white people there, different nationalities, the Germans speak German, the French speak French, and the English speak English. Here,' she said, 'there are the *Pramyayr Naasyoon*,' the Indians, 'there are the Blackfoot, they speak their language, *lii Syoo*,' the Sioux, 'they speak their language, Dakota, the Cree, they speak their *niihiyow* language. Then it was our turn, we are the ones who finish that circle in creation. God gave us *this* language, so we could *all* understand one another, and called it Michif like our nation.'

"If I asked my grandparents what language they spoke, they always said, '*li Krii biikishkwaan, maaka namooya li vray Krii,*' meaning 'I speak Cree, but it's not the real Cree because I use French in my language.' And that's how they'd explain it."

It took less than a century for the new language to take root after first contact between French and Cree, and that rapid formation, said Norman, has brought linguistic experts from Europe to study the language.

"There were these new people who were not this and not that. What are we going to call them? In Lower Canada it was *Mitif*—French for 'mixed blood.' But because of the way the new people spoke, their distinctive accent, they couldn't pronounce the 't,' so they said Michif.

"We inherited our European heritage and our First Nations heritage but became a distinct people. We 'michified' it—the language, the stories, the mythology—all those things became Michif. The Cree word for us, *Otipaymishoowuk*, means 'owners of their own destinies.' The free people.

"When we talk among ourselves, there are no questions of who we are—we know who we are. But it gets lost in translation. Trying to tell your story in another language is not easy."

The prairie we are driving across needs translating, too, though there are words here that belong. The southern edge of the pasture is wrinkled with ravines or coulees on the rim of the Qu'Appelle Valley. *Coulee* is a Michif word that has made its way into modern English in the west.

Down through those coulees and across the river, half a day's walk through speargrass, aspen bush, and slopes of bur oak and bluestem grass, three small monuments mark the national historic site where traders from Montreal built Fort Espérance in 1787. In defiance of the 1670 HBC royal charter granting the corporation exclusive domain over Rupert's Land—all land draining into Hudson Bay—the Montreal traders had followed fur trader Pierre Gaultier de Varennes, Sieur de la Vérendrye, and his sons deep into the interior of the northwest to trade with the Saulteaux (Anishinaabe), Cree, and Dene where they lived. HBC officers soon realized that these "pedlars"—at Fort Espérance and other inland forts—were changing the game. It would no longer work to sit at York Factory on the coast of Hudson Bay and wait for Cree trappers to travel with their furs to the post.

Calling themselves the North West Company (established in 1779), these Montreal traders were among the first people with European blood to walk and paddle the Qu'Appelle Valley. In the early years, they were Michif and French men who resented British control of the territory, but they were soon joined by Scottish men who had their own reasons to hate the English.

When the HBC began to build its own inland trade forts, the competition was on. Employing the toughest men they could find—Métis, Orkneymen, and displaced highlanders—the two companies leapfrogged upstream past one another, striking deeper into the watersheds of the Athabasca, Saskatchewan, and Qu'Appelle rivers in search of furs. In the North West Company (NWC), clans that had feuded for centuries on the far side of the Atlantic—the McKenzies, Camerons, Campbells, and McTavishes—now stood together to face the HBC, their new common enemy that was a proxy for the English king. This new world held the promise of a return to the high and free life of their ancestors, and there would be many a bloody dawn before they let the English take it all for themselves.

By 1804, outposts on the lower Qu'Appelle were exploding and smouldering at regular intervals. The two companies burned out one another's forts with some regularity, seizing trade goods and pemmican and jailing the factors and their men.

The feud climaxed in 1816, when a young Nor'Wester, Cuthbert Grant, left Fort Espérance to guard a pemmican shipment with a brigade of sixty mounted men. Some, like Grant, had Scottish blood mixed with Cree or Saulteaux heritage, and others were descendants of French traders and Cree or Saulteaux mothers. Most would have spoken Michif and one or two other languages.

The men who died that day were the first casualties in a two-hundred-year struggle over how we want the prairie to be used and shared among Indigenous and non-Indigenous people. All the elements that plague our decisions about these lands today were present then: powerful corporate interests, misguided public policy, and groups of disenfranchised people, with long tenure on the land, who are recognized and valued only when it suits the interests of those whose names are on the titles.

The surnames of the men who rode with Grant that morning in 1816 are still here on the Sand Plains and at many other places scattered across the west: Boucher, Hourie, Tanner, Fleury, Lepine, Malaterre, Belhumeur, Pritchard, Falcon, and others. They are etched into gravestones from the Red River to the North Saskatchewan. A few are written on deeds in land title offices.

It is doubtful that many are on papers granting rights to the oil and gas under the soil, but people with such surnames work far afield in those industries today.

The extractive industry that fuelled the passage of NWC and HBC boats into and out of beaver, marten, and mink country relied almost entirely on the hunting skills of Métis, mostly Michif-speaking, men on the prairie. Paddlers on the Athabasca, Churchill, and Saskatchewan rivers were powered by pemmican, the northwest's high-energy staple made of dried and pulverized buffalo meat, mixed with melted fat and berries, and stored in bags made from buffalo hide. Each man working in a York boat or canoe would eat two pounds a day. The easiest way to procure and process the required meat was to open "victualling posts" at the edges of the plains along rivers within a few days' paddling distance of the fur country to the north.

Fort Espérance was one of these depots for extracting and processing transportation fuel. Métis men near the posts were useful as buffalo hunters, and their wives were useful as pemmican processors. They saw none of the profits accrued in London or Montreal by the white owners of the two companies, but they understood that products made from each buffalo could be traded for guns, blankets, pots, sugar, flour, and rum. By 1812, though, the NWC discovered another use for Métis plainsmen—as allies who could be persuaded to fight the corporation's battles.

How little things have changed here in two hundred years. The wild buffalo herds disappeared into the belly of the trade, but the prairie is still a place of depots and posts where cheap food and fuel are gathered to be shipped elsewhere at the bidding of men in distant boardrooms. And the people who live on the land and do the dirty work of producing and shipping the food and fuel are still drawn into fights ignited and ultimately extinguished in those distant rooms.

On the morning of May 8, 1816, when young Cuthbert Grant led his brigade of sixty buffalo hunters east from Fort Espérance, he could not have guessed that the events to come would lead future generations of Métis to place him at the origins of their nation and its fight for an indigenous hold on the prairie or that the violence about to erupt might one day be considered a form of resistance early in the lineage that led to defining Métis' acts of nationhood at both the Red River and the North Saskatchewan.

Grant did know that the new Selkirk colonists at the forks of the Assiniboine and Red rivers were threatening his livelihood and freedom. The colony's appointed governor had posted a law, the "Pemmican Proclamation," placing an embargo on the export of pemmican from the region. That injunction, abetted by a further prohibition against the "running of the buffalo" (the Métis' preferred method of hunting on horseback), made the Métis and their employers in the NWC into allies against a common enemy. A colony pronouncing rules on how pemmican was to be acquired and exported was as much a threat to the nascent Métis plains culture as it was to the business of the NWC.

The company's officers had appointed several of their Métis clerks to be captains but chose Grant to be their "captain general of all the half-breeds." Historian George Woodcock has argued that Grant knew he was being used but took on the role in the hope that it would advance his career in the company. The feud with the HBC had been under way for twelve years or more without any law to dampen the sport. One more skirmish wouldn't hurt.

The Selkirk Colony was a philanthropical side project allowed by the British government at the bidding of the Earl of Selkirk, Thomas Douglas, a man with big dreams who had a seat on the board of the HBC. The Scottish peasant colonists Douglas wanted to bring to the northwest were themselves refugees from another enclosure of the commons across the Atlantic. Allowing them to settle in the chartered lands would be a significant departure from company policy, so Selkirk had to make his case to both the HBC and England's Secretary of War and the Colonies, Lord Bathurst. There were three strategic reasons for allowing a colony of Scottish settlers in Rupert's Land: the colonists could grow food for the company, settlement would improve the value of HBC lands, and settlers would bring civilization to the Indians.

Cheap food to fuel economic growth, a chance to improve value for investors, and managing Indigenous peoples—to this day these are the pillars of federal public policy in Canada's hinterlands.

Norman lets the truck roll to a slower pace as we pass through the gate into the Spy Hill–Ellice community pasture. "I worked on those corrals forty years ago."

Norman grew up among men who made the original fences a couple of decades before he was born. Stalwart trunk and limbs, a full head of curly black hair, and an unguarded smile, he is in his sixties now. As he talks, squinting through the windshield against the sun's glare, I am distracted by the thought that he inherited his stature from buffalo runners whose grandchildren became fence builders.

"It happened in the late 1930s. The Depression. A lot of our people needed work, so when the government decided to make a community pasture here they got some income putting up fences."

When the light improves, we will come back. Branimir has a soft spot for corrals backlit with pink skies, and we are driving through a plain of native grass lit with the fuchsia of three-flowered avens in full bloom. As we reach the far side, the other aspect of the savannah landscape—aspen bush—takes over. A copse of poplar leans out towards the expanse of grass, and our trail draws us into the wall of green it forms. As we approach, an opening in the aspen emerges. Spanned by a gate made of wood and wire painted white, it is unlike any I have seen in a community pasture. This is our destination for the day. Like living ramparts, the poplars encircle a space that, for Norman and the Michif of this region, is filled with all of the story and meaning a place can hold.

"Ste. Madeleine." I look up at the words fourteen feet above the grass in white capital letters formed from steel rods bent and welded to a black frame arching over the gate. In the distance I can see rows of headstones and a large white wooden cross with a Red River cart wheel at its crux, but the sign does not use the word *cemetery*—only *Ste. Madeleine*.

Out of the truck, Norman opens the gate, and it swings lightly on sprung hinges. There are two out-houses on the left and two more on the right. As we walk forward into the ten acres of grass surrounded by aspen trees, something about the place stirs a pang of nostalgia for an old prairie fairground I knew as a kid.

I ask Norman how Ste. Madeleine came to be.

"It was Father DeCorby. He used to travel out with the people on the buffalo hunt. With the Red River people, the ones who were scattered after the first Riel resistance in 1869. The settlers were hostile, so many of our people decided to leave. 'We can go farther west,' they said, 'we know those places from the buffalo hunts. We'll go see uncle, we'll go visit cousin farther west.' Some of them found places to live near Fort Ellice, just south of here.

"He was a good horseman, DeCorby. He came and served the Fort Ellice people when it closed down in the late 1800s. At St. Lazare, just a few miles from here, they built a church together; then a couple of years after that he helped the people living here build one—a mission they called it. That was the beginning of Ste. Madeleine. That's how we got here."

Cuthbert Grant was but twenty-three years old when he led the sixty horsemen east, but he had already seen the colonizers' civilization first-hand at the boarding school he had attended in Montreal.[3] It would spread over the prairie and change everything, the way it had in the St. Lawrence Valley. The pemmican trade fed and clothed every family in the Qu'Appelle and Assiniboine country. If they let that collection of oatmeal eaters at the Red River start dictating the laws of the land, soon there would be farmsteads all over the plains—and, even worse, he'd be stuck on one of them.

Not that his boss, the NWC's Alexander Macdonell, could be trusted either. He was a bastard, just like his cousin Miles Macdonell, the governor of the Selkirk Colony who had the gall to write the Pemmican Proclamation. But Alexander Macdonell was the devil Grant knew.

His official instructions were to escort a shipment of pemmican safely past the colony and into the hands of Nor'Westers on Lake Winnipeg nearing starvation. That much Alexander Macdonell would admit when the gun smoke cleared and he had his chance to testify. Grant, he would say, was told not to threaten or attack the settlers.

No one knows what Grant was actually told before he left. The NWC had been using the Métis to fight its battles with the HBC for twenty years by then. Only three years earlier the Macdonell cousins had begun to argue over who owned the rights to the territory and its resources. Alexander and the Nor'Westers started a campaign of intimidation fuelled by dreams of nationhood that they encouraged among their Métis employees.

It was relatively easy for the Nor'Westers to ship Miles Macdonell and the first batch of Scottish settlers back east, but another group arrived the next year under a governor more foolhardy than the first. Robert Semple, a man more accustomed to the drawing room than the canoe, penned thoughtful essays for the *Edinburgh Review*. Regardless of the vanity or credulity that brought such a dandy to the gunpowdered northwest at this dangerous juncture, Semple set the tone for his brief governorship shortly after arriving in the territory in the late fall of 1815.

On a tour of the District of Assiniboia—as the lands included in the Selkirk concession were now called—Semple arrived at the gates of Grant's fort in the eastern Qu'Appelle. After some presumed niceties, he announced that the NWC must surrender the fort and its supply of pemmican forthwith. Grant, no doubt puzzled by the man's apparent delusion, showed remarkable restraint in not tying Semple to the nearest oak and smearing him with lard. Instead, the record shows that he merely said no and bid him a good day.

The following March Semple managed to seize the NWC's Fort Gibraltar at the Forks, cutting off its trade route north along the Red River. Then he had his men dismantle the fort and float its logs downriver to reinforce the colony's Fort Douglas. This was the sequence of escalating hostility on the minds of Grant and his men when they left the valley in May.

Their first act was to ambush an HBC canoe brigade carrying pemmican down the Qu'Appelle River. It was heading for the Red River to feed the colonists, short on food after several years of failed crops, but now it would be escorted along the Assiniboine River and then past Fort Douglas and the Selkirk Colony to reach the hungry brigades of Nor'Westers waiting on Lake Winnipeg.

Partway along the Assiniboine River, Grant and his men stopped in at Brandon House, the HBC fort just above the point where the Assiniboine receives the Souris River, near today's Brandon. The great Peter Fidler, explorer and cartographer of the northwest, was the HBC factor for Brandon House at the time. Here is his account of the moment when Grant and his troops rode in under their new flag of Métis nationhood, given to them by Alexander Macdonell, a blue horizontal X-shaped cross formed into a sideways figure eight, a variation of the ancient white saltire of Scotland:

> At half past noon about 48 halfbreeds, Canadians, Freemen and Indians came all riding on Horseback, with their flag flying blue about

4 feet square and a figure of 8 horizontally in the middle, one beating an Indian drum, and many of them singing Indian songs, they all rode directly to the usual crossing place over the river where they all stopped about two minutes, and instead of going down the bank and riding across the river they all turned suddenly and rode full speed into our yard—some of them tied their horses, others loose and fixed their flag at our door, which they soon afterwards hoisted over our East Gate next the Canadian house—Cuthbert Grant then came up to me in the yard and demanded of me to deliver to him all the keys of our stores warehouses and I of course would not deliver them up—they then rushed into the house and broke open the warehouse door first, plundered the warehouse of every article it contained, tore up part of the cellar floor and cut out the parchment windows without saying what this was done for or by whose authority—Alex. McDonell, Serephim, Bostonais, and Allan McDonell were at their house looking on the whole time.[4]

Neither Fidler nor his men were harmed, but the message was received: colonizing plans drafted in London by English investors are not welcome in this new world of buffalo, muskets, and grass. Against this and any other incursion stands a new nation, by their mothers native to the prairie, who will defend their claim to the land.

Norman leads us towards what looks like a well-tended campsite. Picnic tables next to a firepit, chairs upturned and stored carefully to one side on a countertop, two large grills made from oil drums cut in half and welded together, and, tucked into the bush, a small school bus up on blocks and converted into a camper.

In front of all this stands a cast iron pump with a wooden handle. Next to the housing is a plastic milk jug half-filled with water. Norman pours some into the top of the pump, and I lever the handle up and down. In ten strokes the priming takes hold, and I can feel the water rise in the pipe from somewhere beneath the yarrow and sage growing at our feet. A couple of hollow glugs, and then water sloshes out in curling ropes of crystal lit by the sun. It smells of earth, tastes of iron, but a cupful in the hand runs cold and satisfying down the throat.

Norman explains the campsite. "The families still come here. Ste. Madeleine means something to us. Some of this was brought here recently I think—it looks new—but there's a celebration here every summer. Ste. Madeleine Days—lots of people, food, music, and dancing. It's like Back to Batoche Days.

"We don't know for sure, but in 1937 they say there were about 250 people living all around here. The plaque in the cemetery says the population peaked at 400 in the '20s. Father DeCorby was long gone, but the church was just over there, and there was a school too.

"It was the 1930s, so times were pretty hard. For the people of Ste. Madeleine, the buffalo hunt, our commercial life, had been gone for a while. Our homeland on the Red River had been taken away. The people who settled here to try farming had moved west after the events there with Riel. There are unmarked graves out here from that first dispersal generation.

"Some of them were already subsistence farmers. They might have had two or three cows, they might have had a team of horses. So they'd look at this place and say, 'Well, let's go there,' because it was all prairie like this. There were a lot of berries here, a lot of herbs, there was water, and there were trees. Everything that they needed. With the poplar they could build their houses, furnish them, and keep warm.

"They came here for deliverance, for freedom, to hold on to a way of life that they were accustomed to. The spring and fall buffalo hunts had to be replaced with something else, so they decided to become farmers. They were the first farmers in the area.

"The light sandy soil had not attracted many white homesteaders, but some of the Métis took homesteads here—most of them did. It was extended families. The farms were scattered here and there on the plains surrounding the settlement. Some of the families did better than others because of their circumstances. If you had a quarter-section of land, you could have five or six families live on it. Just living the old way. But then this whole new way of doing things is imposed. Taxes and land surveys and establishing municipalities with sections and townships and ranges. We'd been here for more than a hundred years, and then this new system just takes over.

"But when we talk about those days, sometimes it sounds like there was always bad relations between the white farmers and our people. But that isn't right. There are lots of stories about them helping one another. When the first white farmers came, they sometimes needed help, and the Métis knew how to survive and showed them things. And then they would help each other, like neighbours do. Sure, there were problems, but it wasn't all bad."

As Norman spoke, I remembered reading that many of the other families would leave the community for months at a time to get work on settler farms in the area. In 1987, Ken and Victoria Zeilig put together a book of interviews with people who had lived in Ste. Madeleine.[5]

One of the longest testimonies came from Harry Pelletier, whose grandfather, Edouard Pelletier, was wounded at Batoche. In his interview, Harry described Ste. Madeleine's farmland and townsite as taking up five square miles "from the boundary of Saskatchewan down to the [Assiniboine] River."[6] In spring, he said, his father would take him and the other children out of school. The family would travel and live in a big tent. The children would cut brush and cordwood while their father worked as a farmhand. They received a dollar and a half for a cord of wood.

Several others interviewed for the book mentioned "scrubbing," or cutting brush and gathering Seneca root, a native plant used in making pharmaceuticals for tuberculosis. Some families would pay a fee for the right to cut hay on Crown land. When winter came, the families would return to Ste. Madeleine, and the children would return to school.

Norman remembers his grandparents disagreeing on the value of a school education. His grandfather saw people being swindled and losing their land because they could not read or understand the legal system. He wanted his children to go to school.

"My grandmother was more traditional, and she said, 'Why?' You see, she didn't go to school. She always said, 'The kids can work like you, they can cut cordwood, they can work for farmers, they can dig Seneca root, they can cut fenceposts, they can haul to the convent and to the stores, and they can make a living like you.'

But my grandfather started to see things differently—he thought we could become educated and be doctors or lawyers."

If a lack of formal education placed Ste. Madeleine and other Métis communities at a disadvantage when white settlers arrived and began offering money for land, the colonial imposition of the Dominion Land Survey and Dominion Lands Act, still fresh in the minds of Elders, set the stage for the landlessness that would characterize the Métis in the twentieth century. The fraudulent land scrip system, to all appearances devised to ensure that very few Métis would actually make their way through its convoluted procedures and retain title to prairie lands, allowed the Canadian government to strip away traditional Métis title and clear the plains for settlement while avoiding the need to negotiate treaties and almost appearing benevolent in the bargain.

The Métis retreated to places like Ste. Madeleine not merely to survive but to hold on to the remnants of their traditional concepts of land tenure, which had been developed locally on the prairie and worked for generations before the northwest was dealt from the HBC to Canada. In his interview, Harry Pelletier said that his parents had each received 240 acres of land through the scrip system established to compensate the Métis after the events at Red River, but his father had sold his land for fifty dollars one day.

Norman begins to walk toward the cemetery, and I follow. Although the community might have once spread over the thousands of acres all around us, Ste. Madeleine as a historic site and cemetery is a hand-ful of acres fenced off from the rest of the community pasture. There are five strands of barbed wire strung high and tight between solid fenceposts. No Hereford is getting through. It would take a buffalo.

A recent grave waiting for its headstone is marked with a small plastic stake noting "Braendle-Bruce Funeral Service." The burial happened last summer, but the sand atop the grave is already being reclaimed by tufts of native grass, small mandalas of antennaria in bloom, as well as chickweed, fairy candelabra, and thread-leaved sedge. None of it would reach the top of my shoes. Asked about management of the cemetery, Norman says that there are so many unmarked graves from the first generation of Michif escaping the aftermath of Red River and Batoche that the funeral service companies sometimes come across bones when they dig new ones.

The headstones bear the same names from those early conflicts. Norman reads them as he passes slowly down a row, stopping now and then to tell a short story of this woman's connection to Louis Riel or that man's ability to speak several Indigenous languages. The names vibrate with cultural pride harkening back to a golden age: David Isadore Genaille, Mary Victoria Demontigny, Ambrose Morrisette, Alfred Laurent, Riel Fleury.

Stopping before the grave of Louis Pelletier, Norman lowers his chin. "I remember old Louis saying, 'It was a good place to live. We lived like we used to live.' That was the way those people talked about Ste. Madeleine. And without saying what that was but meaning we were self-sufficient and still living the old ways even though the buffalo was gone. They define it through the stories they tell you. Hunting and survival techniques, the relationship to the land, the animals, and the birds—the things that were given to them by the creator. My grandparents would always put it that way and speak about what God had given us.

"The people here were resourceful and independent. They knew how to survive. We had good relationships with the winged beings and the four-leggeds. They knew the times for things—when to pick the berries and when not to. You could not find better conservationists. I remember the older people always talking about how everything used to be pure and clean. That is the word they used—*clean*. The water was clean, the fish, the animals. Everything they ate was clean, and they had good, respectful relationships to the land and the other beings, and they knew how to take care of the land and those relationships."

In the middle of the next row, Norman begins to speak of his great-grandfather on his mother's side, Jean-Baptiste Lepine. At the Red River in 1869, he was part of Riel's provisional government asserting the Métis claim on the newly established District of Assiniboia. He sat on the tribunal that tried and convicted Thomas Scott of treason but was one of the two who voted against the death penalty. But Norman wants to talk about Jean-Baptiste's work with Father DeCorby.

"When Father DeCorby went west to establish missions, Jean-Baptiste went with him as a guide because he could speak Cree and Saulteaux. One time they went to La Prairie Ronde (forty miles south of Saskatoon today and contained in Dundurn PFRA pasture) to visit relatives there, the Trottier family. This was quite late, and the buffalo were already disappearing.[7] Anyway, the Trottiers went out on their last buffalo hunt, and my great-grandfather went with them. He told that story to my mother."

Trottier. When I was a kid growing up in Saskatoon in the late 1960s, that was the most feared name on either side of the river. La Prairie Ronde's Trottiers were living in urban poverty by then and had acquired some habits that made them well known and well respected in schoolyards. Behind their backs, we called them Indians. No one told us that they were the great-grandchildren of the last great Métis buffalo hunters or that they were who they were in 1969 because in 1869 our ancestors sold the land out from under their feet.

The first Selkirk Colony farmers used hoes and shovels to tear up the ancient bluestem and cordgrass prairie along the Red River so they could plant their crops. For two or three summers, the seeds they had brought from Scotland failed to produce crops. Rust and other plant diseases, grasshoppers, and harsh weather kept the northern Great Plains' first non-Indigenous settlers hungry and dependent on pemmican and other country food. But there was another threat that made it hard for the hoe-wielding colonists to sleep on spring nights: the possibility that a band of NWC Métis might again chase them away before they could see their crops ripen.

Shortly after Captain General Cuthbert Grant and his party turned inland on the morning of June 19, 1816, to cross the prairie and circumvent the HBC garrison at Fort Douglas, they spotted two Selkirk farmers working the soil. It is not clear from the record, but some reports suggest that Grant's men threatened or intimidated the farmers.

Separating fact from fancy in the reports of an encounter between Indigenous and non-Indigenous people is tricky when it happened yesterday. At the distance of two centuries, that job is mired in a slurry of ideological history-making crafted by interpreters choosing from among various accounts to suit their own larger narratives of how this land became the happy home of white farmers, potash miners, and oil workers.

Grant MacEwan—not the most scholarly of prairie historians but one who knew a good tale and how to supplement it with a flourish of imagination here and there—begins his account with a description of a young settler boy in a watchtower at the Forks. Seeing the mounted brigade approach along the river road, the boy, wrote MacEwan, "gave warning. Governor Robert Semple, showing neither excitement nor emotion, placed the spyglass to his eye and agreed that these were probably the Métis about whom he had been warned."[8]

Gathering a group of twenty-four farmers with guns, Semple marched out to meet the brigade at a place the settlers called Seven Oaks. Mid-twentieth-century historians of Anglo-Canadian descent presented Grant as the aggressor, but more recent interpretations have argued that the Métis did not want trouble and merely planned to escort their cargo safely around Fort Douglas to deliver it to their counterparts to the north on Lake Winnipeg. All accounts agree that Grant initially sent one of his lieutenants, François-Firmin Boucher, to parley with Semple and his band of settlers, all of whom were on foot.

There is no account of what words passed between Boucher and Semple, but it is fair to assume that the governor, enamoured of his commission as the king's representative in this land of heathens, did his best to assert his authority and demanded that the brigade surrender its cargo and retreat. Boucher, as a Métis plainsman with no loyalty to proclamations and principalities concocted by Englishmen on this side of the Atlantic or the other, may well have responded with the nineteenth-century equivalent of "Blow it out your arse, you pompous jackass. You are surrounded by sixty mounted sharpshooters who can kill a buffalo at a hundred paces as they gallop over gopher holes. Put down your guns and step aside."

Regardless of the words exchanged, the next move belonged to Semple. All accounts report that, as the discussion deteriorated into yelling, the governor reached out and grabbed the bridle of Boucher's horse (some say it was his gun that Semple grabbed). At that point someone fired a shot. A pause and then a second shot that set off a barrage of gunfire by both sides. A commission appointed a year later by the British government and led by Lieutenant Colonel William Coltman would conclude that the first shot came from Semple's men, but some witnesses said that two shots came from that side before the Métis moved to defend themselves.

Most reports agree that in the melee Grant shot Semple in the thigh. MacEwan and some other historians describe a moment when the wounded Selkirk governor cried out to Grant for mercy, asking to be dragged to safety. Grant, according to this narrative, turned away to find help just as one of his men rode by and shot Semple in the head. Fifteen minutes later, with the smoke of musket fire drifting over the Red River, twenty-one settlers lay dead among the willows and grass of Seven Oaks.[9] The Nor'Westers had lost but one.

How the battle ended in such a one-sided body count can be explained in part by lack of military experience among the settlers. Métis accounts say that, after firing their first volley, Grant's men fell to the ground to reload their muzzleloaders, as was their custom in battle. The settlers, believing they had hit their targets, threw up their arms and cheered, only to find the dead on their feet and charging at them, muskets blazing. That was when most of the twenty-one died.

Reports divide along ideological lines when historians try to account for what happened next. Someone among Grant's men stripped the bodies of several settlers and mutilated them. Peter C. Newman, that cheerleader for Canadian business from the HBC forward, enthusiastically described it as "an orgy of mutilation."[10] Others, similarly undaunted by the passage of centuries, have taken the accounts of settlers at face value and not investigated them any further.

In 1991, Lyle Dick, a historian working for Parks Canada, conducted an exhaustive survey and analysis of writing by both academic and popular historians who have, since the 1820s, given many interpretations of the events at Seven Oaks. Publishing his paper in the *Journal of the Canadian Historical Association*, Dick identified a shift in perspective over the two centuries.[11]

The popular interpretation of Seven Oaks as a "massacre," as it is still referred to in most history books, did not show up until the post-1870 period, just in time for Canada to justify its dispossession of the Métis and First Nations of the northwest.

For the first fifty years, though, most interpretations offered a more balanced narrative based upon the Coltman Commission's report, representing Grant's Métis not as bloodthirsty savages but as participants in a larger struggle between the Métis and the North West Company on one side and the Hudson's Bay Company and settlers on the other. Coltman's balanced report, based upon sixteen depositions from settlers and seventeen from Métis people, concluded that the only mutilation and desecration of the settlers' bodies was at the hands of a French Canadian man, François Dechamps, and his three sons. None of the Métis in Grant's brigade participated.

From 1870 onward, however, the "massacre-by-Métis" narrative, amplified and repeated by Anglo-Canadian historians, began to dominate. Selecting partisan accounts from settler witnesses, Manitoba historians such as George Bryce, president of the Royal Society of Canada, constructed romantic plots and morality tales pitting a warlike Métis against defenceless settlers, savagery against civility. "Having tasted blood in the death of Governor Semple, they were turbulent ever after," Bryce said in a paper he delivered to an audience of the society a mere ten days after Riel's execution in November 1885. "A too generous Government overlooked the serious nature of those events. It was reserved for what we may trust may be the last manifestation of this unruly spirit existent for three quarters of a century to show itself on the banks of the Saskatchewan in 1885."[12]

Although recent academic interpretations such as Dick's textual analysis have uncovered a more nuanced and complex understanding of the events and their social-political context, a century of Anglo-Canadian history telling has distorted mainstream perceptions of Métis people from Seven Oaks onward, covering up any anterior responsibility settler culture might have for their landlessness and poverty.

A new "master narrative of progress," Dick wrote, required the Métis to assume "broader allegorical roles . . . . The Métis needed to be seen as violent, volatile, easily led astray, and lacking in judgement—in short, as the antithesis of qualities considered essential to the development of a stable free market economy in the West."[13]

Seven Oaks was one of several battles the Métis would win over the next seventy-five years, but the war was one of attrition in which no Indigenous nation could prevail. In the years to come, Grant would learn there was no way to hold back the flood of Anglo-Canadian agricultural settlement loosed upon the plains by the Selkirk Colony.

Before the deluge, however, Grant's Nor'Westers chased away the settlers a second time that summer of 1816. Without harming anyone, they put the Scottish farmers into boats and sent them downriver to Canada. Grant returned to his home in the Qu'Appelle Valley, leaving a few of his men in charge of Fort Douglas. But their grip on the Forks was to last only seven months. On January 10, 1817, Miles Macdonell returned with a small battalion of trained Swiss mercenaries, veterans of the War of 1812 hired by Lord Selkirk, to retake the colony. In the cold light of a winter dawn, they hoisted four ladders against the stockades and went over the top, recapturing Fort Douglas and placing the NWC men under arrest.

Hearing the news, Grant mustered a troop of men and headed east once more, setting up camp at a safe distance. From there he and Macdonell exchanged threatening letters. In one of them, Grant closed with "your threats you make use of, we laugh at them and you may come with your forces at any time you please. We shall always be ready to meet you with a good heart."[14]

Grant, perhaps seeing that this was a battle that he and his men would almost certainly lose, eventually agreed to go peaceably to Montreal to face several charges, including murder. Arriving in October 1817, he waited in a jail cell for his hearing. Some time the next year, while released on his own cognizance, Grant found a light canoe and fled to the northwest. Woodcock speculates that the law in Montreal, home of the NWC, had little love for the English and the HBC and no enthusiasm for pursuing such a fugitive through the wilds to the west.[15]

When the English courts of Upper Canada examined the events at Seven Oaks, the NWC denied any responsibility and blamed Grant. Tried by proxy, he was nevertheless cleared of the indictment.

In 1821, the two fur-trading companies—weary of the fight and losing profits—decided to merge under the HBC name. In a matter of months, they closed one of the two formerly competing forts at all trading centres across the northwest. The HBC, now led by the infamous George Simpson, moved great numbers of suddenly unemployed NWC and HBC men, women, and children to the colony at Red River. These Michif and French-speaking people became the Red River Métis of the great buffalo-hunting brigades. For the next five decades, they grew crops and raised livestock along the two rivers at the Forks and headed out in the spring and fall in their long cart trains to hunt buffalo on the western plains. Some historians would call it the Golden Age of the Métis, but it was launched by unemployment from a corporate merger.

Governor Simpson was the type-specimen for today's sociopathic CEO: shrewd, deceitful, amoral, and utterly dedicated to the monomania of profit making first and last. Within a year of taking his post at the head of the newly merged HBC, he had acquired a chilling grasp of how to use commerce to manipulate and subjugate the Indigenous people in his territory. His journal includes passages that locate the foundations of Canada's abuse of First Peoples decades before treaties and residential schools, in the heart of the fur-trade era, which too often has been romanticized in Anglo-Canadians' telling of history:

> I have made it my study to examine the nature and character of the Indians and however

repugnant it may be to our feelings, I am convinced that they must be ruled with a rod of iron, to bring, and to keep them in a proper state of subordination, and the most certain way to effect this is by letting them feel their dependence upon us. In the Woods and Northern barren grounds this measure ought to be pursued rigidly next year if they do not improve, and no credit, not so much as a load of ammunition given them until they exhibit an inclination to renew their habits of industry. In the plains however this system will not do, as they can live independent of us, and by withholding ammunition, tobacco and spirits, the staple articles of trade, for one year they will recover the use of their Bows and spears and lose sight of their smoking and Drinking habits.[16]

It did not take Simpson long to recognize the utility of a man like Cuthbert Grant. Having been flushed out of the northwest's remote forts and brought to the Red River after the amalgamation, the Métis, Simpson realized, outnumbered the English settlers and could become a source of instability. If he could gain

the cooperation of Grant and convince him to become
a settler-farmer, then other Métis men would follow.
In 1824, Simpson gave Grant a large piece of land at
White Horse Plain along the Assiniboine River, invit-
ing him to establish his own settlement, Grantown (at
today's St. François Xavier). Simpson noted in a report
to shareholders that

> he has got a grant of land at White Horse
> Plain . . . where he is joined by McGillis, Potts,
> Bolinot, Inkster . . . . These people will turn
> their attention to agriculture . . . . I shall rejoice
> if the plan takes as it will rid us of the greatest
> evil . . . . Grant has turned very serious and
> by management will become a useful man to
> the colony and company, but he requires good
> management, being an Indian in nature.[17]

One hundred families followed Grant to Grantown in the first year. That spring he plowed his first
thirty-four acres of prairie. Later he dammed a creek
and placed a water wheel flour mill on the pond, but
it never worked. In 1828, Simpson completed the process of securing Grant's support by employing a tactic that has often served Canadian governments and

corporations well in their dealings with Indigenous people. He invented a title for Grant, appointing him Warden of the Plains, and paid him a handsome stipend of two hundred pounds per annum. Describing Grant in his *Book of Servants' Characters*, a private HR dossier in which Simpson evaluated the utility of more than 170 company employees, he referred to the appointment as "a sinecure afforded him entirely from political motives ... [to prevent] him from interfering with the trade which he would otherwise do in all probability."[18]

Grant lived out his days at Grantown, each spring and fall leading large buffalo-hunting expeditions farther west as the great herds retreated and thinned out year after year. The pemmican they took continued to fuel the transportation of furs and trade goods into and out of the northern reaches of the HBC charter, but the trade shifted over time away from the beaver pelt to the buffalo robe. All fur-bearing animals were in decline from centuries of commercial trapping, but the market was changing too. Silk hats were catching on in Europe, and beaver hats were falling out of fashion, while buffalo hides and robes began to find new markets.

By 1860, the plains had lost both its warden and Simpson, its de facto emperor. Grant, content and no longer a militant, had nothing to do with the resistance that would eventually form among the Red River people. In 1854, he fell from his horse and soon died of complications from the injuries. Simpson, having invested his substantial earnings and dividends in steamship and rail companies, died a very wealthy man on his estate in Lower Canada.

A new era was on its way. Within the decade, the HBC would sell its land charter to the freshly constituted Dominion of Canada for £300,000, without so much as a thought for the rights of the First Nations and Métis peoples. That backroom deal would set off a cascade of policy and exploitation that would exterminate the buffalo and force the Plains Cree, Blackfoot, Saulteaux, and Assiniboine into signing treaties, eventually starving them into submission and onto small reserves. Advancing west from the foothold of colonization at the Red River, the railway would soon release a flood of immigrant, land-hungry farmers with John Deere plows ready to turn the ancient prairie into wheat fields homestead by homestead.

Norman stops at a headstone with the family name Boucher. Could it be a descendant of François-Firmin Boucher, the one who parleyed with Semple at Seven Oaks? Before I have a chance to ask Norman, we are on to another name.

"Alec Venne. He used to talk about the day they left Ste. Madeleine. He said they stopped to look back one more time and saw smoke rising from buildings.

"You see, many of the people were away when it happened, working on farms around Langenburg, or on farms at other places, doing different types of jobs during the summer. They were away from home working, and they came back to find their houses burned to the ground and the town gone."

It was the late 1930s. Millions of square miles of grass had been plowed up, and farmers all over the northern Great Plains had already used up much of the ancient prairie soil's organic matter. Failed crops and too much tillage had left the land exposed to the blowtorch winds of drought. Topsoil built up over thousands of years by the trinity of grass, bison, and fire was suddenly travelling aloft in apocalyptic dust storms. When homesteaders began abandoning their farms, the federal government formed a new agency called the Prairie Farm Rehabilitation Administration.

It would work with rural municipalities and governments in the prairie provinces to stabilize the soil in the worst-hit areas by removing any remaining farmers and then establishing large community pastures that would hold on to the soil and offer affordable grazing to local livestock producers.

In 1937, two representatives of the Rural Municipality of St. Lazare, John Selby and Ben Fouillard, came to Ste. Madeleine and began telling people that they would all have to leave. The land—more than three thousand acres where Métis families lived—was being reclaimed by the federal government to make a community pasture. Those with title and paid-up taxes would receive equivalent parcels nearby. People who did not have title, or those who had title but unpaid taxes, would be resettled with no compensation in one of two new settlements to be established in the municipality. Anyone who tried to stay on the land would be removed by force. And so, most families slowly moved away over the next year, leaving their homes behind. At some point, the municipality men moved in and lit the houses and other buildings on fire. Witnesses say they shot several dogs at the settlement.

Harry Pelletier was away from home working with the Métis Federation in Saskatchewan at the time,

learning about the Métis' historical right to land. In
Ste. Madeleine, Community without a Town, he talks
about his return to the town in 1938: "I just came for a
visit. See how the people were making out . . . . There
was nobody there. A few people still, but that's all . . . .
[t]hey'd moved their houses, their furniture . . . . They
were going to make a pasture and put cattle in there."[19]
When he went looking for his relatives and friends, he
found them in the nearby town of Binscarth and at the
two resettlement sites along road allowances, named—
by the residents and not without some irony—after the
municipal men who had ordered the clearance: Selby
Town and Fouillard Corner. A few were squatting
elsewhere. Many others were missing.

> I found my brother, Louis, living on a farm-
> er's land. I stayed there till winter came. Then
> the war broke out. I went back to Russell
> [Manitoba] and joined the army. I stayed in
> the army till 1946. Yes, everything was lost
> 'cause my place where I was raised was gone.
> And I couldn't find the people. They were scat-
> tered all over the country . . . . I get kind of
> lonesome, wishing to be back again, in that
> place. Because that's where I was raised. We

made our living in there. We had gardens. We had everything we needed there . . . . They pushed us out of our homes and they burned our houses and shot our dogs.[20]

At the end of his interview, Harry tells Riel stories he received from his grandfather, wounded at Batoche in 1885. They are part of the oral tradition Métis people keep alive to honour their kinship with their Red River and Batoche descendants. His last story explains how a disguised Riel eventually surrendered to the "red coats." At its conclusion, he mentions that his grandfather told him that Riel's mother-in-law, Mrs. Bellehumeur, visited Ste. Madeleine. Then he refers to "old Pat Bellehumeur," Riel's brother-in-law, Patrice, as though he was a resident at some point. Finally, he tells the interviewer that he used to know a song about Riel. "I don't know if I can sing it," he says. "My voice is pretty near gone."[21]

We have arrived at the southwest corner of the cemetery. Past a couple of willows, everything looks different. No plastic flowers, no statues, and no modern headstones. Rows of weathered crosses rise from the grass without any inscriptions—no dates and no names.

One area has narrow concrete headstones with pointed ends, also unmarked and leaning in various directions. They appear to be the oldest graves in the cemetery.

"These are the people from the Gambler Reserve," Norman says as we walk. "They have a little reserve just a couple of miles away, but originally they had all this land around here as part of Treaty Four. Most of it was expropriated to be given to farmers. I hear they got a bit of compensation not too long ago."

I ask Norman about the people of Ste. Madeleine. Shouldn't they be seeking compensation?

He pauses, grimacing in a way that lets me know he is choosing his words carefully. "Yes, sure they should, but you see some people were compensated. A couple of families got better land—there's no denying that. Ask the Boucher family. They will tell you. They had paid their taxes, so they were fairly compensated, and they've done pretty well ever since.

"Some other families never did recover, though. It was devastating for them. Sure, the same thing happened to some white homesteaders in the '30s, but the difference at Ste. Madeleine is that it wasn't just individual farmers losing their connection to a piece of land. It was 250 people losing that connection, but also losing their community, their connections to one another.

If your stories are in the land and in your community, and that all gets uprooted and scattered, how do you continue telling your stories? What happens to that, and what happens to your language?

"But the Michif are survivors. It takes a strong back and a strong mind to be a voyageur or a buffalo hunter. There were hardships, but we survived. And we survived the loss of the buffalo economy, the loss of the trade, and we survived every advance of colonization and settlement on the prairie. We survived Seven Oaks, Red River, Batoche . . . ."

Norman doesn't say the words, but they ring in the air above the gravestones: *and we survived Ste. Madeleine.* The graves lovingly decorated by recent visitors, the pump with water in a jug for priming, and the picnic supplies stored for the summer celebrations to come all testify to the unbroken chain of proprietary interest in this place that the Michif people of Ste. Madeleine have sustained for more than seventy-five years since they were removed from the land. Neither Selby Town nor Fouillard Corner has a cemetery. When the descendants of Ste. Madeleine die, most of them are buried here.

Among prairie peoples, the tenacity and adaptability of the Métis are hard to match. A Métis cultural historian once told me that a Red River cart freighter could walk into an aspen bluff in the morning with no more than a sharp axe and some shaganappi rawhide and emerge at sunset with a new cart that, given a stout pony, could carry half a ton of supplies across the prairie.

Something of that bioregional tenacity made it into the twenty-first century even as Canadian governments dispossessed the Métis people and moved them from self-reliance to dependency. The Ste. Madeleines of the prairie world are here at this end of things, where we speak proudly of survival, but at the other end, when the Métis' indigenous hold on the land began to slip, the narrative is about loss. The denouement of the crisis played out at Seven Oaks and other battles across the Great Plains would be the continent's greatest ecological tragedy—the extirpation of the buffalo. Endorsed by corporate and political interests, that loss would ultimately deprive the prairie, and its hunting cultures, of this region's primary bond between its people and the gifts of the grass.

In the 1830s and '40s, with men like Cuthbert Grant leading the spring and fall buffalo hunts west from the Red River country, the Métis pemmican industry shifted into high gear and continued to fuel the HBC fur trade. As the market moved from beaver to buffalo hides and robes, the pressure to take more buffalo intensified. By 1844, the HBC was processing 75,000 buffalo hides a year at posts on the prairie.

In Alexander Ross's eyewitness account of the spring hunt of 1840, the train of 1,210 Red River carts was six miles long. It included 620 hunters, 650 women, 360 children, more than 400 buffalo-hunting ponies, 600 cart horses, and 500 oxen.[22] A three-year-old Gabriel Dumont was among the 1,600 souls heading west that spring from Pembina (along the Red River south of the Forks in North Dakota). After 250 miles, the cavalcade came across its first large herd of buffalo. Within two hours the hunt was over, and 1,375 buffalo were dead. At the end of the two-month journey, the Métis returned with more than a million pounds of pemmican and meat. Ross estimated that they had left an equal amount on the prairie.

By 1850, there were no buffalo anywhere near the Red River. By 1860, they were gone from Turtle Mountain, just east of today's Manitoba-Saskatchewan border. Over the next decade, the buffalo frontier retreated to the Cypress Hills, where Saskatchewan's western border is today.[23]

Although the pemmican trade had all but vanished, by the early 1870s the Métis could see that they were becoming victims of their own success. But there was much more behind the slaughter than fast ponies, breech-loading rifles, and rising demand for hides. The U.S. government was losing its war with the plains peoples but had come up with a new plan: get rid of the buffalo, and the Indians would soon surrender. For Canada, military justification for extermination was not necessary. The politics of expansion, railway building, and clearing the plains for settlement was enough to urge those in power to look the other way as the buffalo faded from history. In 1877, when it was already much too late, Parliament passed the Buffalo Ordinance, a law aimed at slowing down the slaughter, but one year later it was repealed.

By then, Louis Riel had brought more than one hundred Red River families to Montana, looking for buffalo and a life free from the persecution they had suffered at the hands of white settlers after the failure of their provisional government. The last Métis buffalo hunts are thought to have occurred in the Judith Basin area south of the Missouri River, where a remnant of buffalo had survived.[24]

The eight-thousand-year reign of the plains bison was over. You can parcel out blame any way you like, but if there had been no market for pemmican and robes, no eastern industry using tanned hides to turn its wheels, no corporate greed driving the trade from 1780 onward, and no collusion among the governments in London, Ottawa, and Washington, many things might have turned out differently. If they had wanted to, the powers behind the railways, westward expansion, and trade could have put a halt to the slaughter by disabling the export-based buffalo economy driven by colonial-industrial interests. The hunt would have taken its place again at the centre of a subsistence-based economy for plains peoples, who in turn might have had the self-reliance to hold off on signing treaties until they could be sure they would not be losing the prairie and its resources. No reserves, no Indian agents, no pass laws, and no residential schools. That we did not take that fork in the road and instead dispossessed the ancient prairie of its native peoples, buffalo, and grass stands as one of the great tragedies of the modern era.

It is the end of the day, and the sun is low and filtering through aspen leaves as we sit and talk beneath a Métis flag riffling in the breeze. I am afraid I have exhausted Norman with my questions, but I ask him to take us back one more time to the clearance of Ste. Madeleine.

"Prior to 1938, people may have been poor, but they were happy. They still had their independence, their own ways of doing things. After 1938, people were less independent. There was a loss of self-respect and self-determination. When you're kicked out like that, you lose everything."

Not wanting to misrepresent the complexity of the story, Norman again mentions that a few Ste. Madeleine survivors would tell it differently. "You should talk to them. They take a different angle on what happened."

These days some of the most prosperous Métis families near Ste. Madeleine are running Charolais or Angus beef cattle instead of buffalo. Working with what the prairie provides, a family ranching native grass—regardless of bloodlines—is as much a cultural substitution in the grassland world as their cattle are an ecological substitution. Not the same thing by a long stretch, but replacing some of what has been lost.

If Canada had found a way to respect and retain Métis title to portions of the prairie, then there would be more Indigenous families tending our native rangelands in their own ways, operating alongside white settlers. Together, applying a diverse set of land practices and models of tenure, might they have found a way to hold back the tide of cultivation, development, and resource extraction that continues to lap at the edges of the remaining archipelagos of grassland on the northern Great Plains?

Idle imagining now, perhaps, but anyone who has faced the cultural and ecological tragedies of this place is vulnerable to the allure of "what if?" You find yourself sifting through the stories from before the prairie was given over to plowmen. You look for points in our past where you can detect the weight of history lurching towards the colonial dispensation that still degrades prairie life: the first rifle in the hands of a buffalo hunter; the land assessment expeditions sent forth to find a prairie Eden ordained by God to grow wheat; the handshakes of men signing treaties; the memo recommending "industrial schools" for the people living on reserves; the passing of the Homestead Act; and the advance of the railway, penetrating farther west each summer with its cargo of land-starved peasants and scheming speculators.

If I had to choose a single moment in prairie history when things could still have gone either way, it would be this one. Métis storytelling tradition has it that in 1869, when a twenty-five-year-old Louis Riel was one among many Métis farmers struggling to survive along the Red River, a Canadian survey crew arrived at the Forks. They were there to take the measure of the prairie for the patchwork coat of settlement and cultivation it would soon wear. It was October 11. Riel's cousin André Nault came across the surveyors running their chains across a piece of the community's "hay privilege" used by Edouard Marion.

Six months before, the people of the Red River had heard that Canada had somehow purchased all of Rupert's Land, all 1.5 million square miles of it, from the HBC. As outlandish as that sounded, now there were Englishmen driving survey stakes into land that the community grazed and cut for hay.

Nault went to tell others, and soon there were sixteen men on horseback riding towards Marion's pasture. Unarmed, they dismounted and addressed the crew. Riel was one of the younger men, but he knew English. "Stop," he said, "you will go no farther. This land belongs to Monsieur Marion. We will not let you continue."[25]

When the surveyors did not budge, one of the Red River men quietly placed a moccasined foot on the survey chain. Riel and the other men did likewise. Marion's hay privilege was not surveyed that day, but before sixteen years had passed Riel would hang from a gallows in Regina for his part in a series of escalating conflicts that began that day with sixteen Métis men standing on a surveyor's chain.

When I go to the rim of a river valley—the Qu'Appelle, the Assiniboine, the Saskatchewan—and look at the narrow band of native grass left on the slopes between cultivated bottomland and the sea of monoculture above; when I hear white ranchers argue against reintroducing the buffalo to prairie landscapes; and when I think of Ste. Madeleine and the Sand Plains taken from its people, all of my retrospective "what ifs?" turn from looking back on history to face the work of atonement that stands before all prairie people today.

Branimir takes a last photo of Norman walking through the gravestones, and then we offer our thanks and say goodbye. With Norman's permission, we have decided to camp overnight in the school bus at the picnic site and then get up for the sunrise over Ste. Madeleine.

Before he goes, Norman tells us there are bears here. "You see them sometimes at dusk," he says, stepping into his truck, and leaving us with the image of bears in the dark, rambling through the cemetery like fugitives.

The wind down, evening comes on calm and pellucid from horizon to horizon. The poplars surround us—white guardians of the prairie. Notes of Tennessee warblers, an ovenbird, and a Swainson's thrush ring out from the trees and across the headstones. Barn swallows have settled onto the arms of the white cross encircled by the Red River cart wheel. All the ingredients of peace are here—stillness descending from the sky with nightfall, quiet headstones casting long shadows, the day's last notes of birdsong—but an uneasiness invades my thoughts. There is no peace here because there is no justice.

A lark sparrow lands on a headstone, opens its mouth, and fills the air with its jumble of clear, high notes and a glissando of buzzy trills on a lower register. It is the song of one who has travelled from the grasslands of central Mexico to look for a savannah just like this, with sandy soil and sparse grass next to trees.

It sings to claim a place on the prairie, but its title, and that of many other grassland creatures, has been placed at risk by the same failure to reconcile and bring justice to the land.

As the lark sparrow falls silent, the sun slips down to the western edge of the pasture. Time drifts on air currents between the rows of carved stone and concrete. Then all around me, small dollops of gold, blue, red, and green begin to flicker and glow. Most prairie cemeteries have a few recent graves that are well tended, but at Ste. Madeleine the majority are festooned with solar lights and memorabilia to comfort the spirits of those whose bones rest under the grass: flowers of unnatural hue, stuffed toys, small statues of angels or the Virgin Mary, a red Métis sash, a baseball cap. Some of the lights are crucifixes.

Branimir, out on the open pasture photographing the sunset, returns at dark. We walk to the bus, open its rear door, and climb in. Tidy, with rugs covering the floor, it will make a fine bivouac for the night. There are two cots folded up with quilts and a woodstove vented out the side. On shelves and the floor are large margarine pails with "cups" written on the lids in felt pen and boxes marked "assorted plastic cutlery." A stainless steel dogfood bowl waits under one of the half dozen chairs stored against the walls.

After unrolling my sleeping bag across the floor, I look out the windows at the cemetery. All dark now, but through the screen of aspen trees I can see the coloured lights at the graves. As I stare out at the points of green, red, yellow, and blue, something, or a shadow of something, passes across them from east to west. It moves as an animal would, and when it is gone the lights pulse softly again, like lanterns from the windows of a village gone to sleep.

At daybreak, 4 A.M., with thrushes and ovenbirds leading the day's chorus, I awake to find Branimir already gone.

Pumping water from the well to wash and drink, I head back to the graves of Ste. Madeleine to walk through them one last time. The grass is wet with dew, and the low tufts of speargrass look as spiky as sea urchins, with a droplet of water at the tip of every blade. Ants have made mini-doughnuts of sand wherever the soil is exposed. On the slope falling away from the central cross, the purple-red blossoms of three-flowered avens dangle above a matrix of plants, lichens, and club mosses that have held the prairie together for thousands of years. How much longer they can hold out against the pressure to grow crops to feed the growing hordes of humanity no one can tell.

A flash of white catches my attention amid the plain wooden crosses in the Indian section of the cemetery. It's the lark sparrow again. He is showing off his white-bordered tail, fanning it and drooping his wings as he struts back and forth over a platter-sized patch of bare ground. The chestnut feathers on his crown raised and shining in the sun, the charcoal medallion proudly displayed against his white breastplate, he moves like a tiny guard at the gates of a lost kingdom. Pausing in his ceremonies, he lets out a few soft notes of his courtship song and then flies to a willow. As he disappears in the bush, a second lark sparrow flutters up to the top of the adjacent cross. The male then re-emerges with a tiny twig in his bill and flies over to his mate. There, above the anonymous grave, he passes her the twig, and she holds it while he alights on her back, flicking his tail down and to one side. There is a brief flutter of wings, and then he releases her, flying towards the refuge of the poplars.

The lark sparrow does not need a lot to ensure its kind will still be here next year—a bit of open country with sparse grasses, some bare ground and bush nearby, some weed seeds and grasshoppers to eat. Even a messy farmyard will do for the summer. Beyond Ste. Madeleine, the Spy Hill–Ellice community pasture, with its thousands of acres of speargrass and grama grass, is welcoming chestnut-collared longspurs and Sprague's pipits just back from the winter in northern Mexico, and upland sandpipers and Swainson's hawks back from the pampas of Argentina. These birds, and many other grassland creatures, are fussier than the lark sparrow. They need native grassland, large expanses of it, and for that need they have been suffering.

The cascade of ecological destruction that began with the removal of the buffalo and the buffalo-hunting economy, and continued with the tearing up of the prairie and the suppression of fire, has left the remaining islands of native grass vulnerable to a chain of cause and effect that has altered everything from the microcosm of soil biota to the macrocosm of weather patterns under climate change.

Ste. Madeleine's story, nested within one of those islands, is easily filed away as another narrative of colonial violence against the Indigenous peoples of this place, but it is more than that. Yes, something died here, and it would be wrong to forget that. A worse sin, though, would be to miss what made it through the death and loss and not receive the spirit and life of what is still here and worth fostering, nurturing. That other side of the narrative persists in the courtship of the lark sparrow, in the picnic supplies stored in an old bus, and in the Michif to Go smartphone app that Norman developed and released last year.

There will and should be more talk about who must be compensated for past wrongs, who should be granted land, but those conversations too often resolve down to a discussion of worthiness—the kind of worthiness that comes from a quotient of victimhood bound to this or that quantum of blood. If there is a contest for innocence in our centuries-long drama, then the prairie earth will win every time. Compensating the prairie, by restoring our grasslands, wetlands, and rivers to health, is the good work that would reconcile and bind all of us together, but we have scarcely begun to talk about it.

The land, for its part, does not ask for blood quantum or innocence as a measure of worthiness; it asks only for our forbearance, gratitude, and good labour. To meet those expectations would require a community with the responsibility and respect to restore the land's well-being. Instead, we have invented a private morality and a public legality that protect and mythologize the privileges—secured for us by the colonial enterprise—that parcel out the possibility of wealth family by family. To comfort ourselves with these privileges, we need merely look for our names on titles and contracts; but to find and be disturbed by our responsibilities, our portion of care, and earn our place on the prairie, we need to look elsewhere: between the gravestones, in the unjust narratives of our collective history, and upon the sunlit plains themselves.

— PART 3 —

A PASTURE TO SHARE

On the drive back to Regina, my attention drifts into its default mode of watching for birds and assessing the landscape that brings them back in declining numbers each spring. The miles click by bird by bird, field by field, as the Qu'Appelle Valley gives way to the cultivated land south of it leading to the Trans-Canada Highway: blue-winged teal in a channel dug by a farmer to drain a swale that would have supported nesting teal but instead will produce flax or canola this summer; tree swallows trying to make sense of a small mountain of broken trees and willows bulldozed during the winter; a meadowlark singing by a pasture where the cattle have not left enough grass for a nest; and miles of land running off to every horizon where, instead of seventy species of perennial grass and wildflower to support the birds, there are two or three annual crop species and a few European weeds.

I am good at making this kind of complaint. A lot of white people have the skill. Rural or urban, we like to mutter about what other people are doing to the countryside: the man who puts the string of ugly billboards on the road into town next to the auto graveyard; the lakeshore a lurid green with algal bloom from urban sewage; the wild lilies gone where a new landowner has plowed the road allowance; the pesticides hurting everything from honeybees to barn swallows. Each insult that makes the prairie unattractive and ecologically dysfunctional is at the same time an irritant causing tension and disharmony between neighbours and between farmers and consumers.

Whether it is your field of weeds the municipality decides to spray or the neighbour's dog coming onto your property to harass your llama, all of these issues are about the conflict between private and public interest. In place of a useful set of customs and practices, or a system of local governance that might prevent or resolve such disputes by intervening with a sensitive and intelligently administered community interest, we have a legal system with ham-handed laws devised in distant legislatures and rendered inept by underfunded government agencies and monitoring systems. On rare occasions when they actually discover an infraction—someone illegally altering a creekbed, ditching water off his or her land, or cultivating native grass on leased Crown land—the authorities seem to look the other way, apparently reluctant to intervene and enforce regulations that limit land use rights.

The Blackfoot, Assiniboine, Saulteaux, and Cree people of the region have always held their title communally. Historically, there was a fluidity to their system of tenure, in which large expanses of the great prairie commons were held in traditions of occupancy negotiated in relationships and battles among the tribes. That system worked not only because they lacked bulldozers, smartbombs, and a petroleum industry but also because an individual's freedom to take from the commons was always tempered by cultural and spiritual practices stipulating care and restraint on behalf of the community, human and natural, to which everyone belongs.

Retaining only the barest shreds of any such culturally endorsed forbearance, and wielding the

wealth-concentrating tools of individualism and indus-
trialization, the colonizing English could not abide
a commons. Communal title would not serve their
political and agricultural interests. To fill up the west,
thwart American expansionist ideas of crossing the
forty-ninth parallel, and grow grain to fuel the urban
masses in the east and abroad would require nothing
short of the complete alienation of the prairie into the
hands of the Crown so that it could then be subdivided
and parcelled out into small, exclusive holdings.

From the moment when men like John Palliser,
Henry Youle Hind, and John Macoun first gazed upon
the prairie with an eye to agriculture, the non-Indigenous perspective on land has amounted to little more
than an assessment of its human utility. Settler culture and land governance to this day value the prairie
according to its "highest use" and whether it has been
"improved." To "improve" land you must first break
it, strip it of its natural cover. Once that is accom-
plished, higher use becomes possible. The spectrum
of use begins on the low end with "unimproved"—that
is, natural prairie that has no fences or dugouts for
cattle grazing—and climaxes on the high end with
a shopping mall, urban subdivision, freeway, or golf
course. In between, the range of increasingly higher

uses runs from cattle ranching, to gravel production, to the plowing of land to grow tame hay and pasture, to the annual cropping of cereal, oil, and pulse crops, to oil and gas well development, mining, and damming.

This gradient of value by type of use appears on the balance sheets of landowners, rural municipalities, and provincial governments, which peg property tax rates, real estate prices, lease fees, and rebate programs to the highest actual and potential use of property. Every time land changes hands, every time a landowner or farmer reviews his or her finances, every time a municipal councillor looks for ways to cover the costs of road maintenance, land-use decisions drive the accounting. Before long the logic of highest-use economics, coupled with landowners' rights to do what they like with their properties (neighbours and future generations be damned), drives more and more "improvement." Meanwhile, at the lower levels of use, the prairie waiting to be "improved" is left with little economic value to offer those who decide how it will be treated.

That might sound like an indictment of private property, and it is, but each system also has its virtues. Government title recognizes the long-term public interest in the well-being of the land that extends beyond the life span and concerns of any one person or family. Yet there is no denying the independence and democratizing effects that have come from placing small parcels of the prairie into the hands of thousands of single families—though almost all of those hands were male and white. Private ownership, at least at the small freeholder end of the scale, empowers individuals or families to use the land to feed themselves and foster well-being and economic activity for themselves, which will also spill over into the greater economy.

These are two powerful but opposing ideas—the idea of the public good and the idea of private property—but for centuries now they have been at loggerheads for want of a third element to resolve them: the idea of the commonwealth. The Métis of Canada's northwest, with their distinct makeup of Indigenous and introduced ways, understood and instituted the nuances of that third element out of a cultural and spiritual obligation to the creation that provided everything.

Where did that sense of responsibility to the shared well-being of the earth go? It is still alive in the wisdom of knowledge keepers and in their stories, but in extinguishing Indigenous title to the land our colonizing ancestors at the same time disabled all of the systems and traditions applied by First Nations and

Métis people to regulate how the gifts of the prairie are to be used and shared among those who dwell there.

Reparation, reconciliation, repatriation—the work that comes with seeing that "our tipis are held down by the same peg" centres on land and includes restoration of title, but we must also restore Indigenous models of honouring the community interest.

To argue for reparations, the Métis of Ste. Madeleine, Batoche, Red River, and twenty other places across the prairie have no choice but to use their history as a dispossessed people. They might win more land one day and gain title through the same legal process that ran surveyors' chains across the hay privilege in 1869. That would be right and just, and could help to heal the wounds borne in stories of bigotry and persecution[26] in the aftermath of the 1869 resistance, but there is a healing that land repatriation cannot achieve on its own. It will not by itself bring health to the prairie, for it will not in any way compensate the prairie world and its human cultures for another loss seldom spoken of and yet indivisible from the first.

In an economy founded upon private land ownership, we understand the deprivation that comes with expulsion. When we revisit the twentieth-century narratives of loss and dispossession in which the Métis were driven from the scraps of land left over after settlement, we can recognize the injustice. Those removals, though, were merely the aftershocks of earlier detonations that did untold harm to a nascent prairie culture with an emerging civil regard for the land as a commonwealth and for how it is to be used by the community and individuals. At Red River and Batoche, there were casualties for which our histories have done little accounting. One nation or community losing its hold on the prairie is tragedy enough, but in dismissing the Métis way of sharing its gifts we all lost forms of land-use governance that might well have helped us to protect more of the ecological integrity of our rivers, valleys, and plains into the twenty-first century.

For fifty years, from 1820 to 1870, the Métis settlers at Red River communities practised and regulated a system of land use and commonwealth that placed their agricultural and economic lives within a gradient from riverside farm and garden to shared pasturage to open prairie beyond.[27] Behind the river lots at Red River, and surrounding the village and farmsteads at

Ste. Madeleine, there was always the grass shared in a system that held public and private interests in a healthy tension. At Red River it was the *privilège de couper le foin*—"the right to cut the hay"—the hay privilege. It was a unique form of land-use rights applied to the first two miles of unfenced prairie running back from a farmer's river lot. The hay privilege was not exactly a commons. It was a zone of grassland in which the community shared a broad, long-term interest but in which the adjacent farmer held a more particular and immediate interest as the one who, if he followed the community's rules and regulations, possessed first rights to cut hay or graze his livestock there.

The outer boundary of the hay privilege formed a line parallel to the riverfront and four miles back. It afforded some rights to the community but most usage rights to the adjacent farmer. Beyond that four-mile line was the great prairie commons, which the people also used for grazing, haying, and hunting on a first-come, first-served basis. Claiming only their two-mile river lots and the adjacent hay privilege, the people of Red River recognized that the rest of the prairie remained under Indian title.

By 1835, when there were somewhere between two and three thousand cattle at Red River communities, the Métis had their own regulations governing the exact date when haying could begin on the hay privilege and the prairie just beyond. The date varied according to conditions each summer, but anyone who cut hay before the agreed-upon day would be penalized by losing that year's right to cut hay on his portion of the hay privilege.

As the date neared for the first haying on the prairie outside the hay privilege—usually set for late July or early August—the Red River families would travel out to set up camp on the land a day ahead of time. With children, tents, food, and haying gear aboard their carts, they went out looking for the best grass for the winter to come. At midnight each family would claim its piece of prairie according to a set of common practices and rules of fairness. The community would live in a tent village out on the prairie for most of a month, cutting the prairie grass with sickles and scythes. Each Saturday night everyone rode back to the settlement to attend church and do chores on their farms the next day.

Once the winter's hay supply was stored up at home, the community would begin to prepare for the fall hunt and its much farther journey out onto the prairie.

Riel's provisional government was established in part to protect the Métis' distinctive form of land tenure, recognizing three kinds of title: the private farmstead owned by a family, the open prairie owned communally by First Nations but used by all who lived on the land, and the hay privilege, with its mix of private rights for some kinds of use, communal privileges for other forms of use, and regulations governing the commonwealth of both. When the attempt to assert Métis governance failed and the Province of Manitoba was formed in 1870, the Canadian government promised to preserve Métis title and the hay privilege system. By 1873, however, new settlers had placed claims on the hay privileges of Métis farmers, already being described in legal documents as "former occupants." The lieutenant governor at the time, Alexander Morris, threatened to prosecute them for trespass if they cut any hay on their hay privilege lands.[28]

From that point onward, the new homesteading laws imposed by Canada required that the claimant receiving a 160-acre parcel for a ten-dollar fee must plow at least forty acres and erect a building within the first three years. Only men could make a claim, and if they failed to fulfill those two requirements the land became free for another man to claim. The plan worked with breathtaking speed. Within thirty years the prairie was drawn, quartered, and privatized into little squares in which the homesteader held exclusive rights to use the land as long as he plowed up the minimum number of acres. The concept of long-term community interest helping to sustain a balance of the private and the public had been completely extinguished at Red River and in the signing of the numbered treaties. The new prairie dispensation would prove to leave little room for the commonwealth.

For the Michif people who gathered at the turn of the century around Father DeCorby's mission, Ste. Madeleine offered another chance to reconstitute something of the community land-use ethic their ancestors had established at Red River, Batoche, and other places. There was land where they could grow gardens and crops, enough open prairie for them to hunt and gather, trees to cut, and grass for a hay privilege behind the farmsteads. Their descendants might simply describe that arrangement as tradition or "the old ways," but it was more than that. It was a remnant of an evolving system of community-informed land tenure that had been cut down at the Red River just as it was beginning to adapt to the diminishing buffalo hunt and the demands of modern economies and agriculture.

Sixty years after passage of the Homestead Act, the Canadian government began to see the damage it had unleashed upon the plains. Homesteaders on the lightest soils were abandoning their claims, leaving behind crops eaten by grasshoppers and scorched beneath merciless skies. In Manitoba and Saskatchewan, the federal government worked with municipalities to create a new network of community pastures, including the one at the border between the provinces where 250 Métis people were living at Ste. Madeleine in the traditional way.

The federal and local governments at the time chose not to include the people of Ste. Madeleine in discussions on how to conserve the land around their community in a grazing commons. They chose not to include them in discussions of what was to become of their community. None of that is surprising. This was 1937. White settlers would not have been burdened by any consideration that people with generations of prairie living behind them might know something about grazing land and how to share it or that they might have any historical rights worth considering.

If that was a missed opportunity in 1937—to respect and protect a Métis community and its understanding of land tenure—it has come around again today.

Seventy-eight years later prairie people and governments are trying to decide how to conserve the vulnerable grasslands in the decommissioned community pastures, including the one surrounding Ste. Madeleine.

As I write this in the summer of 2016, we are marking exactly two centuries since Cuthbert Grant rode out of the Qu'Appelle Valley with sixty horsemen and a shipment of pemmican. Armed with a modern perspective on the injustices contained in those centuries, the current governments of Saskatchewan and Manitoba have another opportunity to restore a remnant of the Métis commonwealth at the Spy Hill–Ellice community pasture straddling their common border.

The prairie life, a life of great potential, which Grant, Riel, and every Métis leader since them tried to defend, deserves much more than a remnant, much more than a small attempt to recognize and reinstate the legitimacy of the Métis' distinctive way of dwelling here and sharing the gifts of the earth. Although it would only be a start, all of us who live on these contested plains owe at least that much to history, to the scattered people of Ste. Madeleine, and to the land itself.

On islands of grass all across the northern Great Plains—like the sandy pasture surrounding Ste. Madeleine but each with its own distinct history and ecology—the prairie world carries on besieged by the rising tides of cultivation. If these islands make it through another century of our beleaguered tenure, and if some swift foxes, pronghorn, sage grouse, and longspurs make it too, no one will credit the policy that converted the long horizons of grass to small squares of cropland. They have made it this far on the agricultural limitations of the poorest soils and the care of a few who know how to keep the grass healthy.

A woman contacted me recently asking if I would like to see a piece of native prairie that she had come to own. I have had this kind of invitation before, but there was something in her offer that seemed particular, as though she were following a call or principle. She called herself its "bewildered steward" and said "I don't like to think of myself as owning it so much as sharing it."

She went on, speaking from her delight in the beauty of the place, the way the poplars on the river bottom fade into grassy slopes and meadows above, the time she walked to the top and found herself caught in the gaze of a white wolf. As we spoke, though, it became clear that there was something else about the land that she wanted to discuss.

"You see, it's one of the old Métis river lots on the South Saskatchewan. I looked into it and found the name of the family that lived there in the nineteenth century. Later it was homesteaded by white settlers, ranchers, and they looked after it well, but now I have it, and I am exploring what that means."

Reading Diane Payment's *The Free People/Les gens libres*,[29] she came across a passage describing a celebration on the property hosted by the family some time in the nineteenth century between Christmas and New Year's Day. Driven by what she had learned and a desire to do right by the land, she seemed to be searching for a wider embrace, for a way that leads on towards reconciliation with those who had to leave the riverside they loved, fleeing the economic hardship of dispossession and the violence of Canadian law.

She talked about a small cabin the rancher had built long ago, which she was repairing on weekends with the help of friends. The more time she spent there and walking the prairie and riverbank alone, the more she felt that the place was opening her heart, teaching her about the land and how the Métis had lived along the river. She said she has begun to see the elegance, the beauty, of what she calls their "place-based land-use" system.

"I knew a bit of history about the river lot system in Quebec and here with the Métis, but I know a little bit more now. You walk the land, and you can feel how it was a way of governing land use that was communal and completely in relationship to the ecology and geography of the place. The way we have divided up the prairie into squares just seems so wrong. It isolated us from one another and from the land. The Métis system is about place and community. It makes so much sense to be in walking distance from the neighbour's so you can visit and dance and sing and decide things together.

"One day, watching our wide river run to the north, listening to the poplars and feeling the wind, I realized suddenly why they fought and died for their land—not just to defend a place they loved but to defend a way of living on the land that they knew was right. What happened to the Métis at Batoche was an atrocity. People who spoke for their rights of settlement, livelihood, and governance were driven from their homes, raped, exiled, imprisoned. Many died of illness and starvation. I cannot close my eyes to these truths."

So what do you do when you know the name of the family who lived on the river lot whose title now bears your name? When you feel that your privilege to own land has come at the cost of other privileges your race destroyed, privileges more gracefully regulated by a community made of wild and human relationships? You could give it back of course. Doing so might discharge some liberal guilt for a spell, give you a piece of moral high ground on which to stand. I asked her if that was her plan.

"I will work that out, but all I know for now is this: the work of reconciliation we have been called to do is not just for governments and institutions. I can be, I am, part of it, and getting to know this river lot is helping me find others who want to be part of it too. I may just be a placeholder for it, a steward for a time. Private landowners need to be thinking about that, to let go of the sense that land is only about money and wealth. Part of reconciling as people under treaty—and including the Métis who were left out of the treaty but who also had land rights—is to make decisions that are not about money, that will get us thinking about wealth from a broader, community perspective.

"I've asked a Métis woman to be my Elder as I explore these questions about the land. She agreed, and in that first conversation she told me that 'reconciliation means sharing what we have with one another and not taking from one another.' That made sense to me."

In the end, care for the land and a willingness to share its gifts might be the best measure of entitlement. When I stood in the school bus at Ste. Madeleine and watched that shadow pass between the gravestones, I thought about the old *Wiihtigo* spirit in the traditions of Algonquian peoples and the Métis. The *Wiihtigo* is a demonic force often personified as a gluttonous monster whose hunger can never be satisfied. Watching traders gather and ship thousands of tons of meat and hides out of the prairie, the old and wise might well have warned that *Wiihtigo* was taking charge. Today the prairie suffers more than ever under a *Wiihtigo* economy,[30] making it harder for people to hold together the kind of community that supports the private stewardship of our grasslands.

It will not be easy to defeat such a spirit afoot in the land. It takes courageous fools to walk into a dark place, to say, yes, we can find our way through this. Any chance to create an economy that nurtures the prairie instead of devouring it, to break down the garrison holding the wealth of the land and keeping its

First Peoples out, will require us to embrace the best of Indigenous and settler values.

Faint lights glimmer just ahead. A recent Supreme Court decision declared, after a fifteen-year battle, that responsibility for negotiating with Métis and non-status Indians rests with the federal government. No one knows exactly what the decision will mean, but at the very least it has set the table for serious discussions of outstanding Métis land claims.

Meanwhile, the federal community pastures have not all been transferred yet and to date none of the transferred ones have been sold to private interests. They remain Crown land in both Manitoba and Saskatchewan. The new Liberal government in Ottawa has agreed to review the decision and see what can be done to recover something of the conservation element abandoned when the program was cut. Until then hundreds of thousands of acres of old-growth prairie wait for a reversal of policy or a new way to protect them from the forces that degrade and plow grassland.[31]

The foolish and the brave are among us now, prairie dwellers who get up every morning to see what steps they can take in such dim light. Some of them work with radio telemetry and vegetation surveys; some with education campaigns and mailing lists; others with roadside rallies, round dances, and sweat lodges; still others with stories, dances, ideas, and images. Too often they sort themselves out along lines dividing rural from urban, producer from consumer, public from private, Indigenous from non-Indigenous, but somewhere ahead, where the land rises to meet the pipit song that falls from summer skies, there might yet be a place, a sandy plain, where we, sharing one tent peg, can meet and see how the prairie might bring us together.

A SMALL GOOD THING

— AN AFTERWORD —

At the start of this book, Trevor Herriot said that he hoped some small good thing might come of his efforts in travelling to Ste. Madeleine. I hope and I think it has in this small book. But he was worried when he started out. He was worried that in trying to do something good he might trip a few times. I was worried too.

To be honest, there were times when I was uneasy by his questions and by what Trevor wanted from me as we walked around, talking that day at Ste. Madeleine and driving to the community pasture. I became frustrated and upset at times because people have taken so much from us and have said so many things about us that are destructive and untrue.

But I stayed with Trevor that day and talked with him because I did think that his intentions were good and that he was trying to do a good thing, trying to help protect these grasslands and the creatures on the prairie.

Another reason I worried is because there are many ways to tell the story about this time and place and the people, and there are some who might be able to tell it better than I can or tell it differently. Others will also come to write of this history and speak to what happened. But Trevor phoned me that day and asked me to take him there and tell him what I knew. I agreed because, as I said, I believed he wanted to do something good.

I told Trevor about how some of the Michif people fared better than others. Some people did well—they received some land and compensation. But most lost everything. They came home to find everything had been burned down. Local officials had lit their houses on fire and even shot their dogs—some right in front of the children. It was a scare tactic. And so those Michif families had to walk away from that land with nothing. It was hard to recover from that. How do you ever recover from that?

Still, the Michif people keep coming back to the land there. They return to Ste. Madeleine every year. It's an important and sacred place, and they continue to be closely connected to it and care for it.

Yes, Trevor said he hoped some small good thing might come of his efforts in travelling to Ste. Madeleine and speaking to me that day and writing about the place, the community, hoping it would connect to his understanding of how the native grasses have come to be in such danger of being lost forever. And now I do believe some good has come of his efforts and his speaking to me about our history and what the Michif people face today and what they faced in the past.

Let us not forget that there are also many good stories that we—Michif and settlers—share, stories from our past that tell of how the Michif and newcomers worked together. It was sometimes only by helping each other that we got through terrible and difficult times in those days. Michif families and settler families often supported each other. We sometimes forget that. Not every relationship was a bad one between Michif and white families. Many good relationships existed between us.

With the final word in this book, what I most want is for my children and grandchildren to hear about us and of Ste. Madeleine, and as we move forward into the future, I want them to know this: we lost a lot. We were treated unjustly, and understanding this history is crucial.

But it is also important for them to know—to show them—that the Michif people are survivors. We lived well and independently on the land, and we kept good care of it and the creatures on it. Everything was clean because of how we managed and lived, connected to the land and to the winged ones and the four-leggeds. The way we lived meant that the water was clean and pure, and so were the animals. They were clean and pure and healthy. We were good caretakers of the land. We were the stewards. We still are.

And we continue to be survivors and we are success-ful in so many ways now. We are businesspeople and professors and carpenters and ranchers and lawyers and doctors and politicians and teachers and farmers. We are educated in all ways. As I look ahead, I see a bright future for all of our children and grandchildren. We will continue to live and teach the Michif ways, and learn and speak the Michif language, and we will continue to return to and care for Ste. Madeleine and be tightly connected there as a people.

Indeed, just last month, on June 19, 2016, hundreds of our people gathered at the site of the Seven Oaks victory. We came together to mark the 200th anniversary of that fateful day when we emerged as the Métis Nation. We are the best of both worlds—Indigenous and European—unified into a people. Now we all need to strive to create peace, to bridge these two worlds on this land, and it cannot happen without working with Indigenous peoples.

In the Spirit of Michif,
Norman Fleury
July 19, 2016

NOTES

1   Thomas Berry, *Dream of the Earth* (San Francisco: Sierra Club Books, 1988).

2   D. A. Gauthier and E. B. Wiken, "Monitoring the Conservation of Grassland Habitats, Prairie Ecozone, Canada," *Environ Monitoring Assessment* 88, 1–3 (2003): 343–64.

3   Some biographies suggest that Grant had attended boarding school in Scotland.

4   Peter Fidler, HBCA B/22/A119, quoted in Margaret Arnett MacLeod and W. L. Morton, *Cuthbert Grant of Grantown* (Montreal: McGill-Queen's University Press, 1963), 43.

5   Ken Zeilig and Victoria Zeilig, comps., *Ste. Madeleine, Community without a Town: Metis Elders in Interview* (Winnipeg: Pemmican Publications, 1987).

6   Ibid., 137.

7   Norbert Welsh speaks at length about La Prairie Ronde,
     the Trottiers, and some of the last buffalo-hunting
     expeditions in that area in Mary Weekes (as told to her
     by Welsh), *The Last Buffalo Hunter* (Saskatoon: Fifth
     House Publishers, 1994), 37–77.

8   Grant MacEwan, *Métis Makers of History* (Saskatoon:
     Western Producer Prairie Books, 1981), 18.

9   The general area at the time was known to the Métis
     as Frog Plain. Today it has the Scottish name West
     Kildonan.

10   Peter C. Newman, *Caesars of the Wilderness: Company of
     Adventurers, Volume 2* (Toronto: Penguin Books, 1988),
     175.

11   Lyle Dick, "The Seven Oaks Incident and the
     Construction of a Historical Tradition, 1816 to 1970,"
     Journal of the Canadian Historical Association 2, 1 (1991):
     91–113.

12   George Bryce, "The Old Settlers of Red River: A
     Paper Read before the Society on the Evening of 26th
     November 1885," *Transactions* [Manitoba Historical and
     Scientific Society] 19 (1885): 6.

13   Lyle Dick, "Historical Writing on 'Seven Oaks': The
     Assertion of Anglo-Canadian Cultural Dominance
     in the West," in *The Forks and the Battle of Seven Oaks*

in Manitoba History, ed. Robert Coutts and Richard
Stuart (Winnipeg: Manitoba Historical Society, 1994),
n. pag. http://www.mhs.mb.ca/docs/forkssevenoaks/
historicalwriting.shtml.

14   Cuthbert Grant, letter to Miles Macdonell, Assiniboine
River, March 2, 1817, Library and Archives Canada,
Selkirk Papers, MG 19, E4.

15   George Woodcock, "Grant, Cuthbert (d. 1854),"
in *Dictionary of Canadian Biography*, vol. 8 (Toronto:
University of Toronto; Laval: Université Laval,
2003–16), http://www.biographi.ca/en/bio/grant_
cuthbert_1854_8E.html.

16   Frederick Merk, ed., *Fur Trade and Empire: George
Simpson's Journal 1824–25* (1931; rev. ed., Cambridge,
MA: Harvard University Press, 1968), 179.

17   George Simpson, letter to Andrew Colvile, May 31, 1824,
Library and Archives Canada, Selkirk Papers 26–27,
8221.

18   George Simpson, *Book of Servants' Characters*, quoted in
MacEwan, *Métis Makers of History*, 24.

19   Zeilig and Zeilig, *Ste. Madeleine*, 143.

20   Ibid., 143–46, 191.

21   Ibid., 149.

22 Alexander Ross, *The Red River Settlement: Its Rise,
    Progress, and Present State* (London: Smith, Elder, and
    Company, 1856).

23 Travis R. Annette, "Where the Buffalo Roam: Migration
    of the French Red River Métis to Lewistown, Montana,"
    http://www.montana.edu.

24 Ibid., 46.

25 As recounted in the oral tradition.

26 The law that had removed Riel's provisional government
    so effectively and yoked the northwest to the will of
    Upper Canada was somehow powerless to prosecute
    any of the perpetrators—the white settlers who nearly
    killed André Nault or the mob of Orangemen who
    forced Elzéar Goulet into the river and stoned him to
    death. See D. Bruce Sealey and Antoine S. Lussier, *The
    Metis: Canada's Forgotten People* (Winnipeg: Pemmican
    Publications, 1975), 93.

27 Norma J. Hall, *A Casualty of Colonialism: Red River
    Métis Farming, 1810–1870* (Winnipeg: Wordpress, 2015).

28 Ibid.

29 Diane Payment, *The Free People/Les gens libres* (Calgary:
    University of Calgary Press, 2009).

30 Robin Wall Kimmerer, an enrolled member of the
    Potawatomi Nation, coined this phrase, "Windigo

economy," in her book *Braiding Sweetgrass: Indigenous Wisdom, Scientific Knowledge, and the Teachings of Plants* (Minneapolis: Milkweed Editions, 2013).

31   Governments are capable of surprising reversals. In this summer of 2016, a remnant of native grassland that would have been destroyed by a wind energy development north of Chaplin Lake was spared after hundreds of people let the provincial government in Saskatchewan know their concerns.

REFERENCES

Annette, Travis R. "Where the Buffalo Roam: Migration of the French Red River Métis to Lewistown, Montana." http://www.montana.edu.

Berry, Thomas. *Dream of the Earth*. San Francisco: Sierra Club Books, 1988.

Bryce, George. "The Old Settlers of Red River: A Paper Read before the Society on the Evening of 26th November 1885." *Transactions* [Manitoba Historical and Scientific Society] 19 (1885): n. pag.

Chambers, Cynthia, and Narcisse Blood. "Love Thy Neighbour: Repatriating Precarious Blackfoot Sites." http://www.learnalberta.ca/content/ssmc/html/lovethyneighbor.pdf.

Dick, Lyle. "Historical Writing on 'Seven Oaks': The Assertion of Anglo-Canadian Cultural Dominance in the West." In *The Forks and the Battle of Seven Oaks in Manitoba History*, edited by Robert Coutts and Richard Stuart (Winnipeg: Manitoba Historical Society, 1994), n. pag. http://www.mhs.mb.ca/docs/forkssevenoaks/historicalwriting.shtml.

——. "The Seven Oaks Incident and the Construction of a Historical Tradition, 1816 to 1970." *Journal of the Canadian Historical Association* 2, 1 (1991): 91–113.

Gauthier, D. A., and E. B. Wiken. "Monitoring the Conservation of Grassland Habitats, Prairie Ecozone, Canada." *Environ Monitoring Assessment* 88, 1–3 (2003): 343–64.

Grant, Cuthbert. Letter to Miles Macdonell, Assiniboine River, March 2, 1817. Library and Archives Canada, Selkirk Papers, MG 19, E4.

Hall, Norma J. *A Casualty of Colonialism: Red River Métis Farming, 1810–1870.* Winnipeg: Wordpress, 2015.

Kimmerer, Robin Wall. *Braiding Sweetgrass: Indigenous Wisdom, Scientific Knowledge, and the Teachings of Plants.* Minneapolis: Milkweed Editions, 2013.

MacEwan, Grant. *Métis Makers of History.* Saskatoon: Western Producer Prairie Books, 1981.

MacLeod, Margaret Arnett, and W. L. Morton. *Cuthbert Grant of Grantown.* Montreal: McGill-Queen's University Press, 1963.

Merk, Frederick, ed. *Fur Trade and Empire: George Simpson's Journal 1824–25*. 1931; rev. ed. Cambridge, MA.: Harvard University Press, 1968.

Newman, Peter C. *Caesars of the Wilderness: Company of Adventurers, Volume 2*. Toronto: Penguin Books, 1988.

Payment, Diane. *The Free People/Les gens libres*. Calgary: University of Calgary Press, 2009.

Ross, Alexander. *The Red River Settlement: Its Rise, Progress, and Present State*. London: Smith, Elder, and Company, 1856.

Sealey, D. Bruce, and Antoine S. Lussier. *The Metis: Canada's Forgotten People*. Winnipeg: Pemmican Publications, 1975.

Simpson, George. Letter to Andrew Colvile. May 31, 1824. Library and Archives Canada, Selkirk Papers 26–27, 8221.

Weekes, Mary, comp. *The Last Buffalo Hunter*. Saskatoon: Fifth House Publishers, 1994.

Woodcock, George. "Grant, Cuthbert (d. 1854)." In *Dictionary of Canadian Biography*, vol. 8. Toronto: University of Toronto; Laval: Université Laval, 2003–16. http://www.biographi.ca/en/bio/grant_cuthbert_1854_8E.html.

Zeilig, Ken, and Victoria Zeilig, comps. *Ste. Madeleine, Community without a Town: Metis Elders in Interview*. Winnipeg: Pemmican Publications, 1987.

THE REGINA COLLECTION

Named as a tribute to Saskatchewan's capital city with its rich history of boundary-defying innovation, The Regina Collection builds upon University of Regina Press's motto of "a voice for many peoples." Intimate in size and beautifully packaged, these books aim to tell the stories of those who have been caught up in social and political circumstances beyond their control.

Other books in *The Regina Collection*:

Time Will Say Nothing:
A Philosopher Survives an Iranian Prison
by Ramin Jahanbegloo (2014)

The Education of Augie Merasty:
A Residential School Memoir
by Joseph Auguste Merasty,
with David Carpenter (2015)

Inside the Mental:
Silence, Stigma, Psychiatry, and LSD
by Kay Parley (2016)

Otto & Daria:
A Wartime Journey through No Man's Land
by Eric Koch (2016)

ABOUT TREVOR HERRIOT

TREVOR HERRIOT is a prairie naturalist and author of several award-winning books, including *Grass, Sky, Song* and the national bestseller *River in a Dry Land*. He is a grassland activist and a skilled birder. He posts regularly on *Grass Notes* (trevorherriot.blogspot.ca), his web page on grassland culture and environmental issues, and is featured regularly on CBC Radio for the call-in show *Blue Sky*. He and his wife, Karen, live in Regina, and spend much of their time on a piece of Aspen Parkland prairie east of the city.

ABOUT NORMAN FLEURY

Originally from St. Lazare, Manitoba, NORMAN FLEURY is a gifted storyteller and teacher. Dedicated to the conservation and promotion of the Michif language, he has contributed to dozens of language resources. He currently teaches Michif in the College of Education at the University of Saskatchewan.

A NOTE ON THE TYPE

This body of this book is set in ADOBE JENSON PRO. Adobe Jenson Pro captures the essence of Nicolas Jenson's roman and Ludovico degli Arrighi's italic typeface designs. The combined strength and beauty of these two icons of Renaissance type result in an elegant typeface suited to a broad spectrum of applications.

Designed by Robert Slimbach of the Adobe type design team, Adobe Jenson Pro is part of the family of Adobe Originals historical revivals, including Adobe Garamond Pro and Adobe Caslon Pro. With its many OpenType features, extended language support and typographic refinement, Adobe Jenson Pro provides a power and flexibility for text composition rarely found in digital type.

Text and cover design by Duncan Noel Campbell, University of Regina Press.

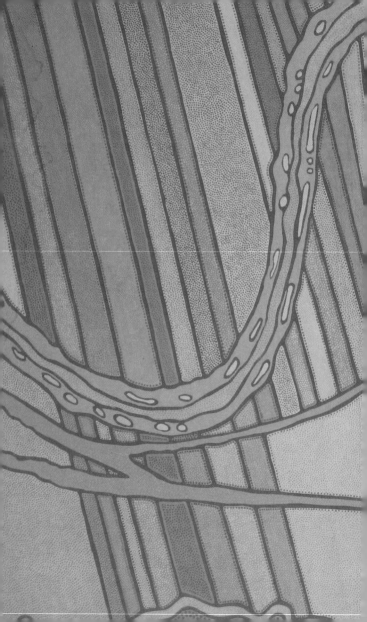